CRO ATIA COAST

DALMATIA DUBROVNIK SPLIT

INSIDER TIP
Your shortcut to a great experience

Travel with Marco Polo Insider Tips

T0066953

MARCO POLO
TOP HIGHLIGHTS

KORNATI ARCHIPELAGO ⭐ 1
The sea dotted with islands around Biograd na Moru is a secluded paradise – ideal for exploring by boat.

📷 *Tip: Don't get too close to the edge of the cliffs when taking a selfie. They are 80m high and have no safety barriers.*

➤ p. 55, Zadar Region

SV. JAKOV CATHEDRAL ⭐ 2
The pièce de résistance of the Dalmatian Renaissance in Šibenik took over 100 years to build.

📷 *Tip: Get the building in one shot by standing next to the statue of its architect, just to the left of the main door.*

➤ p. 59, Zadar Region

VINEYARDS OF PRIMOŠTEN ⭐ 4
The unique winemaking techniques and stunning terraced vineyard gardens produce a distinctive red wine.

➤ p. 63, Zadar Region

KRKA WATERFALLS ⭐ 3
Swimming under the bright green falls in the national park is a heavenly way to cool off.

➤ p. 62, Zadar Region

TROGIR ⭐ 5
This town's palaces, cathedral and walls make it feel like an open-air museum (photo).

➤ p. 68, Split Region

DIOCLETIAN'S PALACE ⭐

Intended to be Emperor Diocletian's retirement home, today the palace is the focal point of Split's old town.

📷 *Tip: Climb to the top of the bell tower for an incredible view (the staircase is worth a photo too).*

➤ p. 71, Split Region

ZLATNI RAT ⭐

This world-famous beach on the island of Brač juts out into the Mediterranean and has plenty of space for sunbathing.

➤ p. 78, Split Region

HVAR TOWN ⭐

Although it's a small port with buckets of tradition, Hvar is also a chic modern hang-out for the wealthy.

📷 *Tip: Pictures taken from the castle above the old town will make all your friends back home jealous.*

➤ p. 81, Split Region

BLUE GROTTO ⭐

If you get there at the right time, this cave on the islet of Biševo will glow like a sapphire.

📷 *Tip: Flash off! You'll lose the magical atmosphere and annoy other visitors if your pics are too bright.*

➤ p. 86, Split Region

DUBROVNIK'S FORTIFICATIONS ⭐

Travel back in time – these chunky bastions once held back pillaging pirates and invading armies.

📷 *Tip: Get some of the windows into the shot to frame your pictures perfectly.*

➤ p. 104, Dubrovnik Region

CONTENTS

CONTENTS

⏱	Plan your visit	🍴	Eating/drinking	🔱	Rainy day activities
€-€€€	Price categories	🛍	Shopping		Budget activities
(*)	Premium-rate phone number	🍸	Going out		Family activities
		🏖	Top beaches	⚑	Classic experiences

(□ A2) Refers to the removable pull-out map
(0) Located off the map

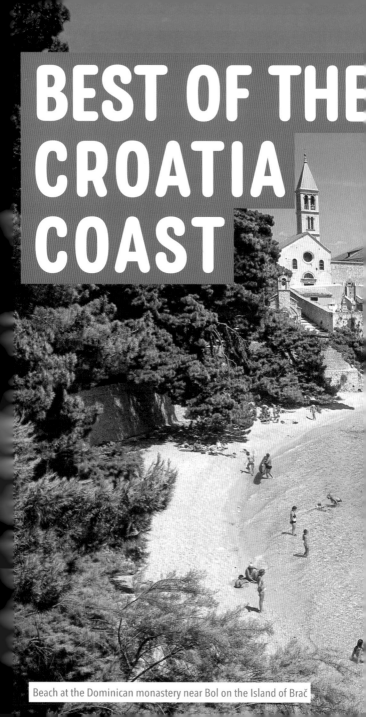

BEST OF THE CROATIA COAST

Beach at the Dominican monastery near Bol on the Island of Brač

BEST ☂

WHEN IT RAINS

ACTIVITIES TO BRIGHTEN YOUR DAY

A SHIPWRECK WITH ITS CARGO

Hundreds of years underwater have not damaged the contents of the Venetian galleon on display in the *Town Museum* of Biograd na Moru. Everything looks as good as it did in the 16th century.

➤ p. 54, Zadar Region

THE FIRST BASE JUMPER

The first man to jump from a tower with a parachute was the Šibenik inventor Faust Vrančić. There is much to learn about this innovative (and occasionally eccentric) genius at the *Memorijalni centar* in Prvić.

➤ p. 61, Zadar Region

A VISIT TO A MAESTRO

Just outside Split's town centre, local sculptor Ivan Meštrović's *Galerija* gives you a taste of 20th-century expressive sculpture and architecture in Croatia. A little-visited serene spot.

➤ p. 72, Split Region

PALATIAL SHOPPING

Any visit to Split's old town should include a stop at *Diocletian's Palace*. While there, enjoy a browse through the craft market in the *Podrumi vaults* (photo).

➤ p. 74, Split Region

THRILLING FORTIFICATIONS

The magnificent *Sv. Ivan Fortress* in Dubrovnik is home to two great attractions: a fascinating aquarium, and a maritime museum explaining all there is to know about ships.

➤ p. 105, Dubrovnik Region

TRENDY TEAMWORK

You can only get out of the *Escape Room* by solving a puzzle, saving a *Game of Thrones* city or finding treasure.

➤ p. 111, Dubrovnik Region

BEST ON A BUDGET

FOR SMALLER WALLETS

A FEAST OF SOUNDS & LIGHTS

Zadar's most compelling attraction won't cost you anything. Spend some time listening to the hypnotic tones of the *Sea Organ* and check out *Greeting to the Sun* (photo), an installation that comes to life at sunset.

➤ p. 44, Zadar Region

MONASTIC TREASURES IN A BEAUTIFUL LOCATION

While most monasteries on the Croatian coast charge entry fees, the Benedictines of *Sv. Kuzma i Damjan*, near Tkon, adhere to monastic generosity and don't charge admission to their beautiful Gothic buildings.

➤ p. 51, Zadar Region

OLD TOWN OASIS

If you want to escape the crowds in Šibenik, pop into the well-hidden and free-to-enter *St Lovre Franciscan Monastery Gardens*.

➤ p. 59, Zadar Region

KEEPING ART IN THE FAMILY

The free *Galerija Jakšić* in Donji Humac has been run by one family of creative Croatians for several generations. They produce stunning sculptures from Brač's famous white, marble-like stone.

➤ p. 81, Split Region

HISTORIC HEADLAND

There is no admission fee to visit the ruins of the *Roman baths* and *Greek necropolis* located on the peninsula near the town of Vis.

➤ p. 85, Split Region

DESCEND INTO THE UNDERWORLD

Dive into the water and discover a dazzling *cave* in which Odysseus is said to have lived for seven years. This adventure on Mljet does not demand any cash or complicated travel … you can get there on foot or by boat.

➤ p. 99, Dubrovnik Region

9

BEST

WITH CHILDREN

FUN FOR YOUNG & OLD

SPIRIT OF ADVENTURE

From water-pistol battles to a huge rollercoaster, the *Fun Park* near Biograd na Moru has a piece of adventure for all levels of bravery.

➤ p. 56, Zadar Region

PARTY WITH THE PIRATES

The Amadria Park resort near Šibenik has sandy beaches and a pirate ship to explore the high seas. There is also an *Aquapark* with slides set up for young kids to burn off all that energy.

➤ p. 60, Zadar Region

FABULOUS FALCONS

Even proud predators sometimes need a helping hand. Ailing eagles, buzzards and peregrines are nursed back to health at Šibenik's *Falconry Centre*, where visitors young and old can learn about these majestic creatures.

➤ p. 62, Zadar Region

UNDER THE SEA

The bright red *Semi Submarines* give you a better panorama of the underwater world than any aquarium. And up on deck the views aren't bad either as you chug past Split's old town.

➤ p. 75, Split Region

WIND IN THEIR HAIR

The channel between Pelješac and Korčula is perfect for little ones to learn the ways of the wind. *Liberan Surfcenter* offers courses for kids up to 13 years old (in a variety of languages).

➤ p. 97, Dubrovnik Region

KIDS TAKE OVER THE TOWN

For two weeks every year Šibenik encourages children to explore their creativity across the city with plays, art, concerts and dance in a variety of venues and with plenty of workshops to teach them new skills.

➤ p. 135, Festivals & events

BEST ⚑

CLASSIC EXPERIENCES

ONLY ON THE CROATIA COAST

A DISTRICT WITH AUTHENTIC FLAIR

The *Varoš* quarter of Zadar's old town is filled with bakeries, hairdressers, cool shops and neighbourhood cafés. At night it transforms into a buzzing bar area.

➤ p. 43 & p. 46, Zadar Region

TASTE THE SEA

Many places in Dalmatia celebrate an annual *Fishermen's night (Ribarska fešta)*, at which all kinds of delicacies from the Adriatic are tried and local people perform traditional dances and plays. One particularly good one is in *Biograd na Moru*.

➤ p. 54, Zadar Region

MONASTIC SEASCAPE

Martinica beach near Bol: a gently curving bay with crystal-clear waters and an idyllic monastery located on the peninsula – Dalmatia at its best.

➤ p. 79, Split Region

BREATHTAKING PANORAMA

The reward for the steep climb from Hvar's *Pjaca* up to the *Španjola Fortress* is a classic Dalmatian panorama: the houses of the old town, a harbour speckled with boats, beyond them the green dots of the *Pakleni otoci* islands floating in the blue of the Adriatic. (photo).

➤ p. 82, Split Region

GET OUT ONTO THE WATER

Make sure to explore *Korčula's old town* from the water. This perspective accentuates its classically Croatian city structure of a cathedral, an episcopal palace and the concentric rings of houses.

➤ p. 100, Dubrovnik Region

SWEET SOUNDS

When the people of Dalmatia sing, they usually do so a cappella and with several voice parts. In July, the best *klapa choirs* head to the town of Omiš.

➤ p. 135, Festival & events

GET TO KNOW THE CROATIA COAST

The island of Galesnjak is shaped like a heart

DISCOVER
THE CROATIA COAST

Stroll along Dubrovnik's beautiful paved streets to Luža Square and Sponza Palace

A coastline stretching as far as the eye can see with thousands of islands dotted along it. Some are inhabited, some little more than jagged reefs. With rugged coves and idyllic beaches, towns built from pristine white stone, Mediterranean flair and historical treasures - it is no surprise dreamy Dalmatia is one of Europe's most popular destinations.

NATURAL WORLD SHROUDED IN MYTH

Dalmatia is one of the four historic regions of Croatia. It covers the area from the island of Rab in the north to the border with Montenegro in the south, including the cities of Zadar, Split and Dubrovnik. Its unique character and beauty have spawned many creation myths. Did God really cry on the bare rocks, whereupon His tears turned into islands? Or did He randomly throw a handful of white

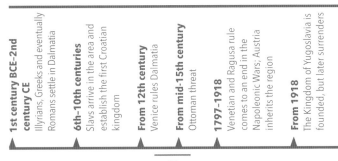

1st century BCE-2nd century CE
Illyrians, Greeks and eventually Romans settle in Dalmatia

6th-10th centuries
Slavs arrive in the area and establish the first Croatian kingdom

From 12th century
Venice rules Dalmatia

From mid-15th century
Ottoman threat

1797-1918
Venetian and Ragusa rule comes to an end in the Napoleonic Wars; Austria inherits the region

From 1918
The Kingdom of Yugoslavia is founded, but later surrenders

pebbles onto the coast which just happened to fall into this beautiful formation?

It is no accident that the Adriatic Sea is the most common subject of local traditional *klapa* music – it is the centre of everything in the region. The era of great seafarers may be over but the Venetian ports they created still gleam along the coast here. Even away from the coast, water is the most important element in the Dalmatian landscape. Rivers chart their course through deep gorges in Paklenica National Park and the Cetina valley; water tumbles over limestone steps at the Krka waterfalls, and the azure blue of the Plitvice Lakes dazzles the senses. If you like hiking and climbing, biking or kayaking, the landscape here will be your idea of paradise.

LIFE IN A MUSEUM

The history of the Croatian coast is like an adventure story that you cannot put down. The past pulses through the walls of palaces, cathedrals and ancient ruins and is given new life with a huge, historically themed festival every year. At Diocletian's Palace in Split you are intimately surrounded by nearly 2,000 years of history and are constantly reminded of its trials and tribulations with the Roman columns and vaults, and the pre-Romanesque stone relief in its baptistery – evidence of an era when Croatia was an independent kingdom and when it opened up to Christianity. There are Gothic carvings on church doors, which were made when Venice subjugated most of Dalmatia. And there's the

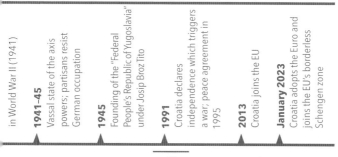

in World War II (1941)

1941-45
Vassal state of the axis powers; partisans resist German occupation

1945
Founding of the "Federal People's Republic of Yugoslavia" under Josip Broz Tito

1991
Croatia declares independence which triggers a war; peace agreement in 1995

2013
Croatia joins the EU

January 2023
Croatia adopts the Euro and joins the EU's borderless Schengen zone

Baroque frenzy of the cathedral's interior, which celebrates the region's golden age. The modern era is also represented here. The people of Split like to while away an hour in the peasant peristyle of the Café Luxor, enjoying an espresso and reading the paper. Only the ancient Greeks failed to immortalize themselves here, but they left their mark elsewhere. On the sea floor, for example, hundreds of amphorae from sunken merchant vessels create archaeologists out of amateur divers. Today life here is not always so idyllic as the scenery suggests with corruption, societal stagnation and unemployment driving many young Croatians to other EU countries in search of a better future. However, tourism on the coast is still booming and makes Dalmatia one of the country's richest regions.

A BLESSING & A CURSE
Swimming in crystal-clear waters is just one of the highlights of the region. Dalmatia is the proud home to a number of UNESCO World Heritage Sites, both cultural and natural: Diocletian's Palace in Split; the Plitvice Lakes; the plain of Stari Grad and its old town; Sv. Jakov Cathedral in Šibenik; Trogir's charming old town; and, since 2017, the last traces of Venice's Dalmatian defence system at Sv. Nikola's fortress in Šibenik as well as Zadar's defensive wall. Not bad, right? But there is still something missing from this list. By far the most famous Cultural Heritage Site here is the impressively well-preserved old town in Dubrovnik. As though designed for a film set, the stone houses within its defensive walls have been extensively used by the producers of *Game of Thrones*. It was once Ragusa, an independent seafaring and trading republic, which resisted the Venetians and the Ottomans with a combination of guile and smart negotiating. Today Dubrovnik is partly a victim of its own success as hordes of tourists disembark from planes and cruise ships every summer thanks to its modern status as a 'must-see' destination. Hvar has a similar problem – a 'place-to-be' for every celeb from the A to the Z list; it can be a bit overwhelming.

ADDICTIVE DESTINATION
It would be hard not to fall in love with a country whose people are so proud of what they see as the world's prettiest corner. Bluer sea, better olive oil or grander history? Pretty much nowhere else. At the very least after a day exploring Split's palaces or Dubrovnik's ancient walls, or after walking through olive groves, or after completely forgetting the daily grind while drinking a glass of wine in a traditional *konoba*, you'll catch yourself thinking that the locals are right. Start exploring! The peaceful charm of the coast with its clear water and picturesque medieval ports, the excellent food served in attractive restaurants, and the beaches with their relaxed party culture will soon win you over.

AT A GLANCE

856,800
Population of Dalmatia

Glasgow: 635,640

942
Islands, islets and outcrops off the Dalmatian coast

1,200km
Length of mainland coast

Welsh coast: 1,400km

12,951km^2
Surface area

Dalmatia makes up 22% of Croatia's total area

HIGHEST MOUNTAIN: DINARA
1,831m
Ben Nevis: 1,345m

HOURS OF SUNSHINE PER YEAR
2,600
UK: 1,493 hrs

MOST POPULAR MONTH TO TRAVEL:
AUGUST

8 UNESCO WORLD HERITAGE SITES
Including the old towns in Dubrovnik and Trogir, and Diocletian's Palace in Split.

SPLIT

Largest Dalmatian city, with 167,100 inhabitants

MOST POPULAR FIRST NAMES
Ivan
Marija

3 CROATIAN BREEDS OF DONKEY: 2 FROM DALMATIA, 1 FROM ISTRIA

UNDERSTAND THE CROATIA COAST

DOWN TO THE CELLAR

Konoba originally meant a cellar or a cool ground-floor room in which food and wine was stored. Today the word refers to the cosiest places in the whole of Dalmatia: small, charming taverns which serve as local social hubs and demonstrate the best of the local hospitality. They are decorated lovingly but sparsely with wooden tables, checked tablecloths and fairly outdated decor which ranges from ancient agricultural tools and musical instruments to paintings of the sea. They mostly serve simple regional food, wine and *rakija*. In theory any pub can call itself a *konoba* but you will spot the most authentic ones from the locals enjoying a glass of wine after work. Once they have had a few more, they may start singing! *Konoba* is also the root of the word *konobar*, which means waiter.

GONE WITH THE WIND

In a country of sailors and islands, wind is not just a matter for everyday chit chat. Wind and its strength are an integral part of life for Croatians. The mighty *Bora* wind makes its presence felt especially in autumn and winter, when it is capable of bringing the country to a standstill: ferry services stop, streets are blocked and towns along the coast get a deep clean. It blows in from the northeast reaching speeds of up to 200kmh (for the sake of comparison, hurricanes start at 118kmh). Don't go near the sea when the Bora is blowing as its ferocity is not only capable of casting ships far out to sea, it has even been known to catapult coaches into the water. Other winds include the *Maestral* and the *Jugo* or *Scirocco*, less known perhaps but equally treacherous. The northwesterly Maestral is said to bring bad weather with high waves and a lot of spray. On the other hand, the Scirocco from the south is not only supposed to blow in sand from the Sahara, but also a depressive mood across the land. In the city-state of Dubrovnik, the wind was once a mitigating factor in the courtroom – offenders were said to receive a milder punishment if the Jugo was blowing when they committed their crime. More dangerous than all these winds put together is the dreaded draught. This may sound eccentric but is taken deadly seriously in the entire southern Slavic region and every child is warned of its perils. Illnesses, diseases, mood swings, family problems can all be attributed to the fact that two windows were left open and a draught was blowing…

LIVE, BREATHE, EAT FOOTBALL

While driving towards Split you will notice a name written on almost every bare patch of wall, on the sign above the local baker or printed large on beach towels. *Hajduk Split* is Croatia's oldest football club, founded in 1911 and worshipped by the locals. The arch-enemy of every genuine Hajduk fan is *Dinamo Zagreb* and the legendary rivalry between the two clubs has been known to break out in violence over the years. For this reason, never walk around Dalmatia sporting Dinamo colours unless you're looking for trouble. Hajduk fans, especially the infamous hooligans who belong to ultra group Torcida, are reportedly linked to far-right ideology and often wear T-shirts sporting the German phrase "Hajduk Jugend" (Hajduk Youth), which has obvious connotations with the Hitler Youth. This fanatical love-hate relationship over football has its limits though: when forest fires raged near Split in the summer of 2017, fans of Hajduk Split and of Dinamo stood side by side to fight the fire.

VIRUS-FREE ZONE

It's well-known that the spotted 101 dogs from the famous Disney film got their name from Dalmatia. But did you know that the word quarantine was also coined here? It was at a time

The Bora wind acts like a deep freeze here on the Makarska Riviera

Dubrovnik's city walls are a must-see for most tourists

when the autonomous city-state of Dubrovnik (then known as Ragusa) was making a name for itself as one of the most important trading and shipping posts in the region. As such, its citizens were exposed to all types of viruses and diseases from around the world. In the battle against the plague in the 14th century, the first quarantine camps were set up in Dubrovnik to contain the rapid spread of the Black Death. The word "quarantine" comes from the Italian word *quaranta*, or *quaranta giorni*, meaning forty days, the period that all passengers were required to be isolated in camps. One of these camps, called the *lazareti*, still stands today, not as a hospital but as an events space and exhibition venue for local artists.

HIGHLY SKILLED TRIO

Everyone has heard of the Italian Renaissance artists such as Michelangelo, but what about Juraj Dalmatinac, Nikola Firentinac or Andrija Aleši? Perhaps not, but they are some of the foremost artists of the Dalmatian Renaissance. In Venetian times, Dalmatia was dominated by Gothic architecture and if the conservative councillors had had it their way in the 14th and 15th centuries, it would have stayed that way. They rejected point blank the ideas of the rebellious youth and the new emerging style – until this trio set the Renaissance movement rolling in Dalmatia with their Italian, humanistic influences. The Dalmatian trademark is an eclectic mixture of old and new: Gothic blends seamlessly with Renaissance. As Juraj Dalmatinac's Italian name Giorgio da Sebenico (1410–75) indicates, he came from Šibenik. However, he began his career in Venice where he worked on buildings including the Scuola di San Marco. In Dalmatia he designed multiple palaces and the cathedral altar in Split, the cathedral in Šibenik (which has a statue of him), and the fortifications of Dubrovnik. His colleague, the Tuscan Nikola Firentinac (Niccolò di Giovanni Fiorentino, 1418–1506), imported the style of his homeland to Dalmatia and collaborated with Dalmatinac on Šibenik Cathedral. He may indeed have introduced Dalmatinac to Renaissance ideas. A frequent third collaborator on significant projects was Andrija Aleši (Andrea Alessi, 1425–1505), a prodigiously talented sculptor from Albania, whose best-known works include the side chapel in Trogir Cathedral – a joint effort with Firentinac. The works of these three masters dominate the architectural landscape of towns in Dalmatia to this day.

LONG LIVE THE ISLAND KING

Today, in the 21st century, the whole of Croatia is a Democratic Republic. The whole of Croatia, you say? Think again! One village on the island of Iž is populated by a group of loyalist Dalmatians who refuse to relinquish

TRUE OR FALSE?

THE ISLANDS ARE IDYLLIC

Many city dwellers spend their days dreaming of Croatia's remote islands. But unreliable connections to the mainland, water shortages and loneliness can make island life decidedly less idyllic. When the Bora blows and the ferries are cancelled, an island can feel as far away as Mars.

EVERYONE LIKES TO SING

"He who doesn't sing … Is not a Dalmatian", or so says the famous song *Večeras je naša fešta* (Our festival is tonight). Even the smallest event is an excuse for a party here. And no party ends without some sort of sing-song.

the monarchy. Located between Dugi otok and Ugljan, this small island off the coast of Zadar clings to its tradition of appointing a new king every year at the end of July. At this folk festival, known as *Iški kralj*, last year's king and his entourage are sailed into the harbour of Veli Iž. The king bids farewell to his loyal subjects to the sounds of fireworks, bells and celebrations. The new king is then elected and inaugurated with performances from choirs, folklore dancers and a big party. The role of king is purely symbolic and the ritual does not mean that the islanders wish a return of the

Habsburg monarchy or the former Croatian kings – the practice goes back to Roman times. Iž was the only island to hold on to the tradition until the 19th century and the revived it in the 1970s as a folkloric festival.

MUSIC FOR THE SOUL

At first, the music of Croatia's *klapa* choirs might seem sentimental and mawkish but you will fall for their charm when you hear them played in a local *konoba* (taverna) while sipping a glass of wine. It doesn't matter if you don't understand the lyrics – they are always about sailing, love or the homeland … or a mixture of all three. Decent *klapa* singers virtually flirt with the sea when they sing. Fans of the music are not really interested in the words. The word *klapa* actually means "group" or "community" and their lull-aby songs invoke a nostalgic image of the Dalmatia of old when the only troubles were catching fish and heart-ache. Although traditionally it is the men who sing, women and mixed choirs are now increasingly popular. The a cappella singing is sometimes accompanied by a type of mandolin, known as the *tamburica*. Some more famous groups such as *Klapa Intrade* and *Klapa Cambi* from Split have man-aged to combine the sound of *klapa* with pop and sometimes appear with Croatian pop stars or cover their hits.

BEAUTIFUL (CLEAN) BEACHES

A picturesque white beach, a shady spot among the pine trees and peb-bles under your flip-flops: the region's beaches are Dalmatia's gold. The only obstacles are the sharp rugged rocks and the sea urchins – but don't panic, simply invest in a pair of jelly shoes. Although sea urchins may not be high in the popularity stakes, these prickly creatures are a good sign because they are only found in clean water. Fine pebbly beaches can be found all along the Makarska Riviera but you will struggle to find real sand anywhere! Between you and me, sandy beaches are overrated. Pebble beaches provide snorkelers and divers with gloriously clear under-water images instead of sandy fog. And it is not only boastful locals who praise the cleanliness of the Adriatic. Many beaches here proudly fly the blue flag.

STUBBORN HELPERS

Before there were tractors, donkeys did the heavy lifting in vineyards and olive groves. Most have now been forced into unemployment (often simply released). However, the sanctu-ary at 🐵 *Tribuni Tovar* offers many a rosier retirement. And some enterpris-ing people still make money from these beasts of burden. Donkey farms such as 🐵 *Dar Mar* in Poljica bring the tourists in and their donkey milk is highly prized as a superfood. In Tribunj the donkeys are part of a much-loved local spectacle when they race around the town centre. A few of them stick to form every year and refuse to join in the fun. In fact, they can behave like divas here as Tribunj has erected a life-size bronze statue to them. With all this attention, it is no surprise that donkeys often grin out at

Sea urchins: a sign you are in clean water

you from Dalmatian postcards – an unlikely symbol for the region.

TYING A KNOT IN MEN'S FASHION

If France lays claims to being the mother of fashion, then Croatia is its grandmother, or the great step-aunt at least. The reason is that the tie originated here. According to legend, in 1663, while the Palace of Versailles was under construction, King Louis XIV of France ordered a parade of troops in front of the building site. Marching alongside the regiments were Croatian mercenaries, whose chests were decorated with cloth rosettes attached to their collars. Louis was so impressed with this accessory that he decreed that his nobles should wear it too, and thus the *cravate* (derived from the French word *croate*) set out on its journey towards global popularity. Although it's true that the word "cravat" is derived from "croat", the rest of the story is almost certainly fiction.

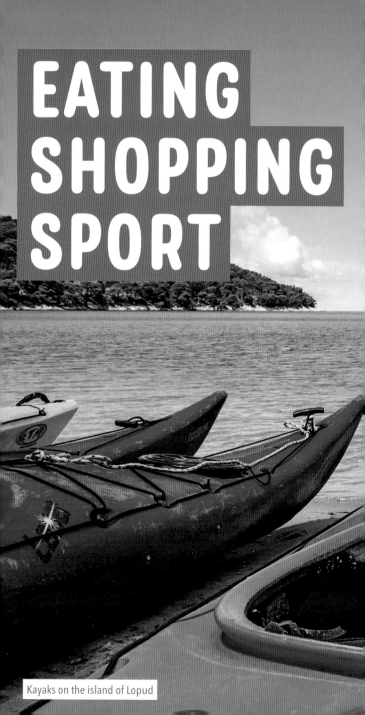

EATING
SHOPPING
SPORT

Kayaks on the island of Lopud

EATING & DRINKING

Ingredients for a traditional Dalmatian dish: to start with, take care and time browsing the fresh produce at the market. Marinate your choice of ingredients in olive oil, herbs and salt. Add a touch of regional flair and finally put the whole lot on the barbecue. Enjoy the results with a sea view, a glass of wine and a shot of Mediterranean relaxation. *Dobar tek* (Bon appetit)!

MEDITERRANEAN CUISINE?

Dalmatia's cuisine is light, nutritious and healthy. It is no surprise that this Mediterranean food was added to UNESCO's World Heritage list in 2013. The Italian influence is very much present, but most things you eat will be regional, and every area has its own way of preparing them. Fresh fish, vegetables and herbs, such as rosemary, sage and thyme, alongside extra virgin olive oil are the basis for most dishes. Heartier meat dishes, pasta and risotto round off most menus.

THE CULINARY CLOCK

Breakfast is the most important meal of the day? Dalmatians, like lots of southern Europeans, don't necessarily agree. They will knock back a coffee *(kava)*, normally in espresso form with a bit of sugar, but eating generally starts with *marenda*, a kind of early lunch, when many restaurants sell cheap snacks such as *rižot* (risotto) or *girice* (whitebait). Bakeries also sell filling snacks such as pizzas and pastries. Dinner is the main meal of the day and is eaten late (8–9pm), once the heat of the day has begun to dissipate.

SIT DOWN, TUCK IN

There are fish restaurants, pizzerias and *konobas* (traditional taverns)

Croatian specialities: *fritule* (left) and fish (right)

everywhere, all serving traditional Dalmatian food. You can tell the quality of a restaurant by how much olive oil they use – the more, the better – there can never be too much. You will always be served soft white bread with your food whether that be chips, pasta or indeed a sandwich. It is at least normally free. There is very rarely a service charge and most locals tip about 10% in a restaurant (no need to do so in a bar). If you want to eat fish, be a bit careful as menus often show a per kilo price. Ask your waiter roughly how much a portion weighs so that you won't be too shocked by the bill. And always get a glass of wine with it. Water with fish is frowned upon here.

FISH & MEAT

Your journey into local cuisine could begin with a starter of a few slices of *pršut*, a thinly sliced air-dried ham often served with olives and sheep's cheese. Most mains involve barbecued fish or meat with vegetable rice or *njoki* on the side. Fish usually comes with *blitva* – steamed chard and potatoes. Mussels, squid and prawns are also staples either grilled or in stews and risottos. Popular meat dishes include *pašticada*, a kind of braised beef, or the Bosnian kebab favourites *pljeskavica* and *čevapčići*. Make sure you try a very traditional local speciality: meat or squid cooked with herbs and vegetables in the embers of a fire in a *peka*, or cast-iron bell. It takes about two hours so you will need to pre-order but it is definitely worth the wait. If you want to try something a bit more unusual, head to the Neretva Delta and try their eel and frog stew. Once this was considered peasant food, today it is highly prized (and priced).

INSIDER TIP
Freshwater food

GREEN & LOCAL

Dalmatians are rightfully proud of their local produce. They stick to regional and fresh food but this does not mean things are organic (if they are, they are often expensive). Vegetarians will find plenty to eat in a vegetable and pasta-rich cuisine. Vegans might find it more difficult although most bigger towns have decent veggie spots. At the very worst you may have to build your own meal from side dishes, where rice and grilled veg are staples.

WINE & DINE

It is no accident that wine is one of the main themes of *klapa* music. Dalmatia produces excellent local tipples and many of its leading winemakers offer tastings of their wares. The red wine *Plavac* is produced along the coast while the Pelješac Peninsula is responsible for *Dingač* and *Postup* wines. Primošten makes *Babić* wine using an indigenous grape.

Desserts are often accompanied by a sweet *Prošek*. This comes in many colours but is not like prosecco (despite Italy's attempts to ban the name given their similarities). If you like a spritzer, order a *gemišt* (white wine) or *bevanda* (red).

If you like your drinks hoppy, give *Ožujsko* or *Karlovačko* beers a try, and if you want a digestif, try a local brandy, or *rakija* (locally these are rumoured to cure all ailments). Drinks menus will always include a range of fruit *rakijas* and the grappa-like *lozovača* as well as the herby *travarica*.

If you're not a drinker, you can order mineral water (*gazirana* if you like it fizzy) or *cedevita* – an immensely popular orangeade.

SWEET TOOTH

Most Dalmatian desserts follow the maxim 'less is more' at least when it comes to the number of ingredients. Most simply use eggs, flour and sugar. This does not make them any less addictive – *fritule* (doughnuts) and *kroštule* (pastries) will soon have you salivating. Restaurants also often serve ice cream, fruit and pancakes.

Traditional *peka* pots are placed in the embers for slow cooking

Today's Specials

Starters

DALMATINSKI PRŠUT
Finely sliced air-dried ham

PAŠKI SIR
A hard sheep's cheese from the island of Pag

SALATA OD HOBOTNICE
Fried squid in a salad

Main courses

PAŠTICADA
Braised beef in a sauce sweetened with dried figs

PEKA
Cast-iron pot used to cook meat or squid in the embers of a fire

JANJETINA
Lamb, often prepared in a *peka*

PLJESKAVICA
Grilled kebab, sometimes filled with cheese *(kajmak)*

CRNI RIŽOT
Black squid-ink risotto

RIBLJA PLATA
Mixed fish grill, which might include sea bream, sea bass or shellfish with chard on the side

Desserts

FRITULE
Small unfilled doughnuts dusted with sugar

ROŽATA
Dubrovnik's take on a crème caramel, often served with *arancini* (candied orange peel)

TROGIRSKI RAFIOLI
Ravioli-shaped pastry filled with almond; a Trogir delicacy

Drinks

DINGAČ
Traditional red wine from the Pelješac Peninsula

MARASCHINO
Liqueur made from marasca cherries from the region of Zadar

LOZOVAČA
Wine brandy, much like grappa

SHOPPING

Every suitcase has a bit of space to bring some souvenirs home, and they don't have to be cheap tat either. Spend a bit of time browsing in order to find unique products from exciting local artists and artisans. Or take back a taste of the region.

TOTALLY LOCAL

Some of Split's younger generation have come up with very modern takes on traditional Dalmatian *souvenirs*. Đeloza Dizajn *(FB: delozadizajn)* makes T-shirts with Dalmatian sayings and cool logos. They depict the locals' supposed customary stubbornness with the phrase *"Uvik kontra"* (always against) and a fish swimming in the opposite direction to the rest of its shoal. *Omiš Originals (short.travel/ kkd10)* also produces fun designs: "Local Vocal" is one of the best – a Minecraft version of a *klapa* singer.

Luka Mimica *(FB: blootal)* from Split makes little Adriatic islands from sand and synthetic resin.

SOUVENIRS WITH CLASS

If you want stylish and practical souvenirs that won't be forgotten as soon as you get home, you could try an item of clothing and keep that holiday feeling going. Instead of buying mass produced T-shirts, find a local designer and get something unique – it can be surprisingly affordable. Lots of galleries sell cool and fashionable accessories alongside artworks. And sometimes they turn traditional items into something timeless, such as elegant necklaces made from the marble-like Brač stone or delicate replicas of ancient jewellery made in silver or gold. Some villages sell bags in traditional patterns made from natural fabrics.

INSIDER TIP
Traditional totes

Lavender bags (left) and red wine (right), a speciality of the Pelješac peninsula

SCRUMPTIOUS SOUVENIRS

You can never go wrong with food, and there is plenty of fabulous produce to discover in Dalmatia. How about some fig and orange jam or the Dubrovnik speciality of *arancini* (candied orange peel)? Then there is the local staple: excellent olive oil, which can come flavoured with anything from garlic to herbs and is often sold in elegant glass bottles (if you like that kind of thing).

DRINKS TO DIE FOR

When it comes to wine, brandy and liqueurs, you can often try before you buy. Pelješac red wines are available in the supermarket but it is much more fun to go direct to the producers. Be careful if you're buying homemade *rakija* – not every amateur

distiller knows what they are doing. The most popular brandies around are the grappa-like *lozovača* and the aromatic *travarica*. And if you like your booze sweet, try *medica*, a honey brandy, or the cherry liqueur *maraschino*.

THE SCENT OF LAVENDER

The lavender fields on Hvar are not just photogenic, they are also the source of fragrant souvenirs, which can be found in shops all over the island. As well as the usual soaps and scented bags, you'll find lavender honey and lavender sea salt. You can also try lavender ice-cream – although you won't be able to pack it in your luggage! But a lavender-filled neck pillow should guarantee a calm journey home.

SPORT & ACTIVITIES

With a landscape like this, there is no excuse not to get out and enjoy it. From underwater reefs and high cliffs to excellent paths and great sailing, there is something for everyone.

CANYONING, RAFTING, CANOEING & KAYAKING

A trip down the Cetina, upstream of Omiš, is a must for fans of whitewater rafting and can be booked through a number of providers, such as the *Omiš Rafting Club (tel. 021 863 161 | raft.hr)*. The landscape in the Cetina Gorge, with waterfalls and large pools set among high chalky cliffs, is perfect for canyoning. You can book a trip down the canyon that includes plenty of refreshing dips – or the more extreme version that includes abseiling – with agencies such as *Adventure Dalmatia (Matije Gupca 26, Split | tel. 091 182 8995 | splitadventure.com)*.

The Krupa and Zrmanja rivers in North Dalmatia are popular with canoeists, and a five-hour trip through the rapids of the Zrmanja down to its mouth in the Adriatic can be booked with the agency *Kornatica (Put Slanice 7 | Murter | tel. 099 243 7323 | kornatica.com)*. If you prefer to race down the river in a raft, then visit the *Riva Rafting Centar (Obrovac | tel. 023 689 920 | rivarafting-centar.hr)* near Zadar. Sea kayaking is particularly enjoyable in the Elaphiti archipelago and the Kornati National Park. You can hire kayaks in any of the larger tourist resorts or join a guided tour. On Korčula, for example, this could take you from Lumbarda to the neighbouring islands of Vrnik and Planjak. The provider *Korčula Ventures (Lumbarda 44 | Lumbarda | tel. 098 344 182 | korcula-adventures. com)* also rents out glass-bottomed kayaks.

Drop anchor and dive in! Dalmatia is a boating paradise

CYCLING & MOUNTAIN BIKING

Whether you're into road racing, mountain biking, electric bikes or just pootling, you will find a fun ride in Dalmatia. Dedicated cycle paths are marked out in many places – some of which run along old shepherd paths. The app *Zadar Bike Magic* will give you plenty of options in the area around Zadar with a total of 86 routes covering 3,000km. Local tourist information offices also produce cycle maps to download.

Bike and mountain bike hire is available in most tourist resorts (including electric bikes). Island hopping is particularly good fun on two wheels: travel from island to island by boat and explore the different attractions and landscapes on an off-road bike. Various agencies can help organise these trips (including on e-bikes).

DIVING & SNORKELLING

Thanks to its many small islands and reefs and incredible biodiversity, the Croatian Adriatic is a paradise for divers and snorkellers. You can see fish, crabs and octopuses even when snorkelling from the beach. However, the pros head to places like the Toronto shipwreck near Dubrovnik, the Blue Cave near Biševo or the ancient underwater museum near Lastovo (there are over 100 excellent dive sites in the region). If you join a guided diving trip then you won't need a diving permit. Solo diving is only permitted with a Diver's Card, avalable from a harbourmaster's office if you present your diving certification (approx. 320 euros/year). Information: *croatia.hr*.

FISHING

The rich diversity of Adriatic fish (also freshwater fish as in Lake Vrana) really reels in the fishermen. You need a one-day or multi-day licence which can be obtained from local tourist information offices, or online at *ibarstvo.mps.hr*. A day permit costs around 8 euros and a three-day permit around 20 euros, depending on the location and the gear you use.

HIKING

The walking in Dalmatia is unbelievably beautiful even if you do have to contend with poorly marked paths. However, the national and nature parks, the Biokovo mountains, the island of Mljet, the canyons of Paklenica and Plitvice all offer visitors a wide selection of well-signposted trails. More touristy islands such as Hvar and Brač are also well mapped out. Make sure you stick to marked paths – there are still a few mines left over from the Yugoslavian War.

PARAGLIDING

If you're not afraid of heights, there are great gliding routes in the Split region around Hrvace and near Makarska in the Biokovo mountains. At the moment, the only company offering organised flights in the region is *Paragliding and Hanggliding Dalmatia (tel. 091 619 4723 | FB: Paraglidinghanggliding)* based in Hrvace, about 40 km from Split.

RIDING

Galloping through a coastal landscape, the wind running through the horse's mane – it's a dream that can easily become a reality. In Sinj, 35km from Split, you can live out all your cowboy ambitions in stunning surroundings. Agencies and clubs like the *Riding Club of Split (Radunić, Donje Ogorje | tel. 021 663 555 | equestrianclubsplit.com)* will help organise multi-day trips in Sinj or around the Plitvice lakes.

Beginners will be better suited taking a short hack in the area around Zadar. *Horse Riding Zadar (Hrvatskog Sabora, Zadar | tel. 091 724 9939 | horseridingzadar.com)* has plenty of options and offers ponies for children.

ROCK CLIMBING

Scrabble up sheer rockfaces, test your own limits and best of all get amazing views of the Adriatic coast: climbing is currently very popular, with new routes and areas popping up all the time. The Paklenica National Park is the classic destination on the coast, with rock faces up to 1,600m high and 360 routes ranging in difficulty from 3

to 8b+. Boris Čujić's multilingual climbing guide *Paklenica* has the best information and is available from the Paklenica National Park authority *(tel. 023 369 155 | np-paklenica.hr)*. At the end of spring the International Climbers Meeting – a freeclimbing event – takes place here in the spring. It's an amazing spectacle whether you climb or not.

INSIDER TIP
Pro climbers

The steep slopes of the Cetina Gorge near Omiš *(Tourist-Info Omiš (tel. 021 861 350 | tz-omis.hr and climbingomis.com)* offer very varied climbing. Hvar and Brač are the most popular islands for climbers.

SAILING, WINDSURFING & KITESURFING

With 1,184 islands and 1,777km of coastline, Croatia is a sailing paradise with plenty of small coves and idyllic spots to cast anchor in. The infrastructure for sailors is also superb, with fully modernised marinas and harbours. Contact the *Croatian National Tourist Office (UK tel. +44 208 563 7979 | croatia.hr)* for information on the 56 marinas and their rules. *The Adriatic Croatia International Club (aci-club.hr)* maintains a number of marinas in Dalmatia.

Wind- and kitesurfers regularly congregate in the following areas: Orebić, where high speeds can be reached in the channel between Korčula and Pelješac when wind conditions are favourable *(orebic.hr)*; the strait separating Bol on Brač from the island of Hvar *(bol.hr)*; and Nin to the north of Zadar *(surfmania.hr)*.

Climbers in Paklenica National Park

REGIONAL OVERVIEW

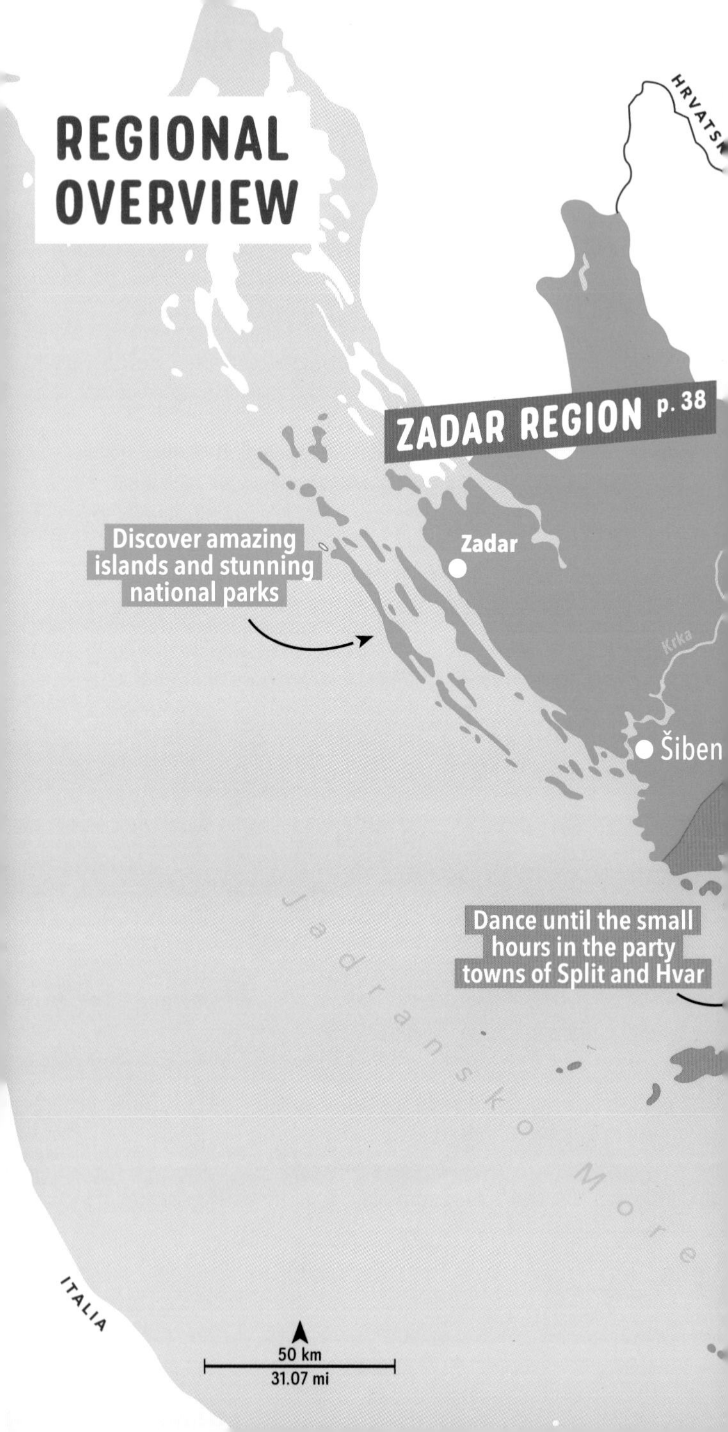
HRVATSK
ZADAR REGION p. 38
Discover amazing islands and stunning national parks
Zadar
Krka
Šiben
Dance until the small hours in the party towns of Split and Hvar
Jadransko More
ITALIA
50 km
31.07 mi

BOSNA I HERCEGOVINA!

Neretva

Split

SPLIT REGION p. 64

DUBROVNIK REGION p. 92

Dive into history in the footsteps of great seafarers

Dubrovnik

CRNA GORA

ZADAR REGION

A TREASURE TROVE OF CULTURE & NATURE

A unique mix of landscapes and cultural treasures from every period of history make northern Dalmatia – between the Velebit mountains in the north and the peninsula village of Primošten in the south – a great destination for a holiday.

As well as the proud ports of Zadar and Šibenik, where Romanesque churches and Renaissance palaces stand alongside modern architectural delights, you can visit the beautiful green waterfalls in Krka National Park, the Paklenica gorges which tunnel deep into the

Bridge over the Krka river

Velebit mountains, the olive groves in Zadar's green suburb, Ugljan, and the cliffs at Dugi otok.

However, it is the thousands of islands in Kornati National Park that are this region's most unforgettable feature. According to legend, the islands were created by God's tears. In reality, the peaks of hills pop out of the Adriatic from a landscape that was submerged during the ice age.

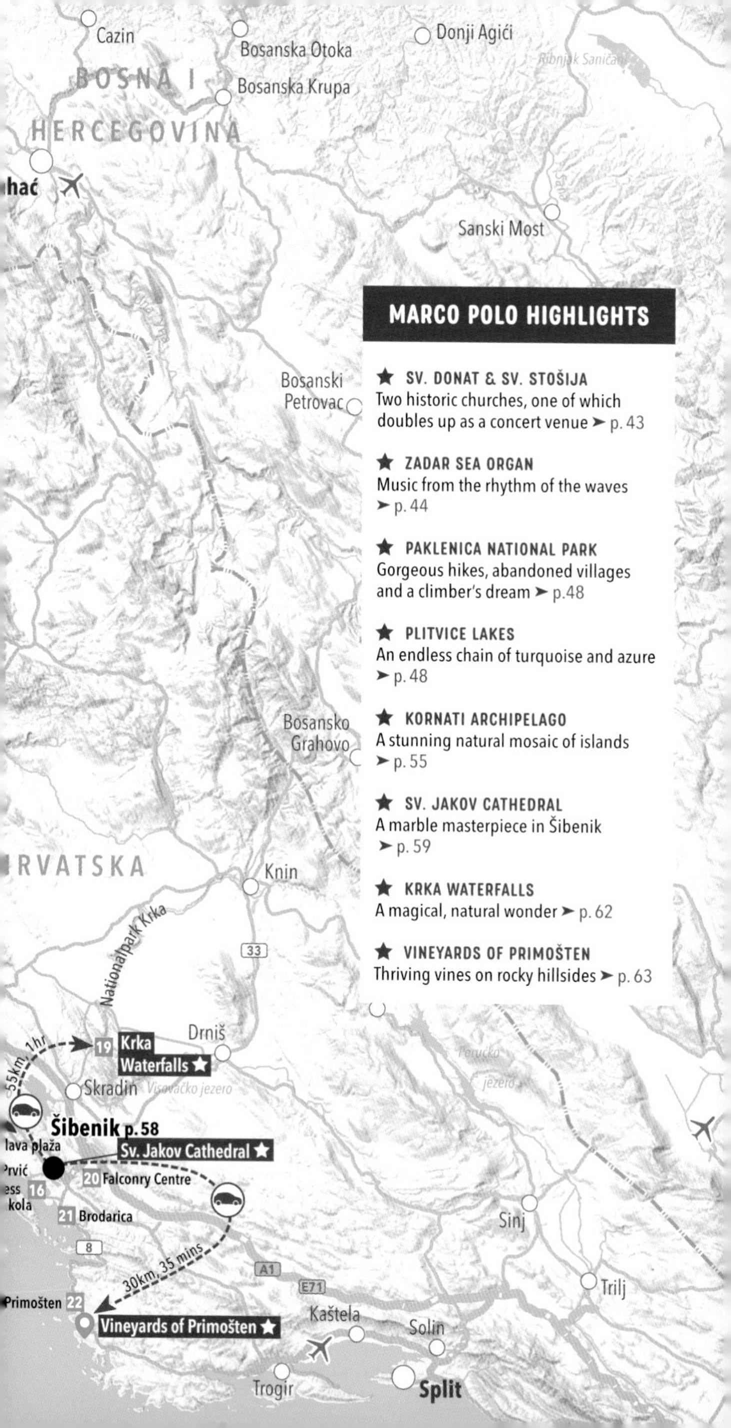

This map shows various locations in Bosnia and Herzegovina (BOSNA I HERCEGOVINA) and Croatia (HRVATSKA), including cities such as Cazin, Bosanska Otoka, Donji Agići, Bosanska Krupa, Sanski Most, Bosanski Petrovac, Bosansko Grahovo, Knin, Drniš, Skradin, Šibenik, Primošten, Sinj, Trilj, Kaštela, Solin, Split, and Trogir.

Nationalpark Krka

33

19 **Krka Waterfalls ★**

Drniš

Skradin   Visovačko jezero

35km, 1hr

Šibenik p. 58

lava plaža

Sv. Jakov Cathedral ★

Prvić
ess
kola   16

20 **Falconry Centre**

21 **Brodarica**

8

A1   E71

30km, 35 mins

Primošten 22   **Vineyards of Primošten ★**

Kaštela

Solin

Split

Trogir

Sinj

Trilj

ZADAR

Dalmatia's second-largest port (pop. 73,000) preserves three millennia of art and architecture, including the city's more recent history – and we don't just mean the enchanting art installation of the *Sea Organ* and the *Greeting to the Sun*, where the city's inhabitants gather to watch the sunset.

Zadar's old town lies on a peninsula, connected to the mainland by a thin strip of land. From 1409 the city was expanded under Venetian rule into a naval fortress complete with walls and towers. Zadar was the capital of Dalmatia until 1918 and its culture was strongly influenced by a large Italian community until 1947, when they left the city after it became part of Yugoslavia. This Italian flair can still be felt today in the city centre, with its many cafés. Amid the Baroque and Gothic houses in the narrow streets of the old town there are plenty of examples of *Razionalismo*, the Italian architectural style of the Fascist period, which were built during the 1920s and 1930s when Zadar was an Italian exclave. British and American bombing raids destroyed much of the old town in 1943 and 1944.

The *Zadar Card (about 8 euros/ day | zadarcard.com)* offers discounts at many sights, shops and restaurants including on a boat trip to the Kornati National Park (there are cheaper multiday options and family discounts).

SIGHTSEEING

PEOPLE'S SQUARE (NARODNI TRG)

Zadar's People's Square is a hub of activity until late in the evening. The old town's central square is lined with a Baroque *Loggia* (16th century), the Renaissance *City Guard* building, and the 19th-century *City Hall*. The foundations of the 11th-century *Sv. Lovro* church are preserved in the *Café Lovre* and, a few steps further on, you can see the attractive *Ghirardini Palace* in Venetian Gothic style.

SQUARE OF THE FIVE WELLS (TRG PET BUNARA)

In the past the only way to reach the peninsula was to cross a drawbridge and pass through the still-intact *Land Gate* (1543), built by Michele Sanmicheli in the form of a triumphal arch. Behind the gate lies the enchanting *Trg pet bunara* with its five Renaissance wells, beneath which Zadar's largest cistern used to collect rainwater. You can still see parts of the crenelated medieval *City Wall* here, along with a watchtower and two beautiful *palaces* from the 14th and 15th centuries. In the Baroque *Sv. Šimun* church, two angels support the imposing gold and silver sarcophagus of the city's patron St Simeon (14th century). To the northwest of the square ⚑ is the lively district of *Varoš* with its narrow bar-filled lanes. There are some old workshops between the many watering holes.

INSIDER TIP
Where Zadar's students drink

GLASS MUSEUM (MUZEJ ANTIČKOG STAKLA)

Playing with fire is fun to watch in this museum where you can see how glass jewellery is moulded from a liquid mass. The well-made replicas of Roman cups, bowls, perfume bottles and lamps are sold in the museum shop. *Mon-Sat 9am-9pm | about 4 euros | Poljana Zemaljskog odbora 1 | mas-zadar.hr | ⏱ 1.5 hrs*

SV. DONAT & SV. STOŠIJA ★

From the remnants of columns and temple foundations it is obvious that this square with its two churches used to be a Roman forum. The idiosyncratic rotunda of the *Sv. Donat church (daily 9am-7pm; June 9am-9pm; July and Aug 9am-10pm | about 3 euros)* was built in the ninth century. At 26m, this pre-Romanesque building is unusually tall; its superb acoustics are put to excellent use during the *music evenings* (see p. 135) held here in the

(see p. 135)

WHERE TO START?

From the waterfront promenade **Obala kneza Branimira** in the new town (where you will find parking) a footbridge will take you to the peninsula and the historic town centre. Keep going straight to get to **Narodni trg**, where you will also find the tourist information. However, a far nicer option is to travel across the harbour from the *barjakoli* in a rowing boat (less than 1 euro) – an 800-year-old tradition.

summer. Inside, the remains of Roman columns and capitals are preserved alongside old Croatian reliefs. Next door, Zadar's *Sv. Stošija cathedral (summer Mon–Fri 8am–2pm, 5–7pm, Sat/Sun 8am–noon; otherwise Mon–Fri 8am–noon, 6–7pm, Sat/Sun 8am–noon)* expanded the city's holy centre in the 12th and 13th centuries. Its Romanesque/Gothic architecture and elegant rose windows are reminiscent of Tuscan churches, while its interior contains three naves and lavishly decorated altars. Of these, the altar with the sarcophagus containing the relics of the church's patron St Anastasia is of particular note. This dates from the ninth century and is decorated with interlaced ornament and a relief depicting the saint. The 56-m bell tower *(June–Sept Mon–Sat 9am–10pm; April, May and Oct Mon–Sat 10am–5pm | about 2 euros)* offers superb views over the old town. | ○ *1 hr*

ARCHAEOLOGICAL MUSEUM (ARHEOLOŠKI MUZEJ)

Start at the top and work your way down chronologically through Zadar's history – from the Illyrians to the Romans, Slavs and the early Croatian Middle Ages. The spectacular exhibits include sarcophagi, baptismal fonts and shrines dating from the 9th to the 11th centuries. The museum shop sells handmade jewellery often replicating archaeological finds. *July/Aug daily 9am–10pm; June and Sept daily 9am–9pm; April/May and Oct*

INSIDER TIP
Roman fashion

Mon–Sat 9am–3pm; Nov–March Mon–Fri 9am–2pm, Sat until 1pm | about 5.50 euros incl. admission to Sv. Donat | Trg opatice Čike 1 | amzd.hr | ○ 2 hrs

GOLD & SILVER OF ZADAR (ZLATO I SREBRO ZADRA)

This *Benedictine monastery* contains an exhibition of fine and ornately decorated religious treasures from across Dalmatia. *Mon–Sat 10am–1pm, 5–7pm, Sun 10am–1pm; winter closed Sun | about 4 euros | ○ 1 hr*

ZADAR SEA ORGAN (MORSKE ORGULJE)

Zadar's favourite meeting point among both locals and tourists is the product of a redesign of the harbour on the westernmost tip of the 500m-wide peninsula. As well as the modern ferry terminal, architect Nikola Basić designed a stylish waterfront promenade with steps running down to the sea. Under the steps are a number of plastic tubes of varying length, each with a pipe attached to the end. Depending on the rhythm of the waves, these pipes produce noises that are sometimes eerie, sometimes contemplative and occasionally they recall the song of a whale. The installation is rounded off by the *Greeting to the Sun (Pozdrav suncu)*. This is a disc made up of 300 glass plates that store energy in their solar cells during the day, before releasing it at night in the form of colourful lights that are triggered by people's footsteps on the disc. Most of the power generated is used to power nearby streetlights.

Remnants of the Roman Forum are visible in front of the 1,200-year-old Sv. Donat church

EATING & DRINKING

BARBAKAN 🐟

A buffet in the former citadel – great value and an epic location. *Rudera Boškovića 5 | tel. 023 300 970 | €*

HARBOR

Bits of old boats, dark wood and metal grates give this restaurant an interesting mix of the rustic and the industrial. Excellent fish, burgers and ribs by the sea with a great view of the old town. *Obala kneza Branimira 6 A | tel. 023 301 520 | harbor.hr | €€*

MALO MISTO

A typical Dalmatian restaurant with a long menu and friendly service. You will see plenty of locals eating here too. *Jurja Dalmatinca 3 | tel. 023 301 831 | malo-misto.com | €€*

PET BUNARA

This restaurant close to Five Wells Square boasts a romantic setting for its creative Dalmatian specialities such as ravioli with scampi or the typical local fig sauce, *šinjorina smokva*. *Ulica Stratico | tel. 023 224 010 | petbunara. com | €€€*

SHOPPING

MARKET (TRŽNICA)

Zadar's lively market sees fruit and vegetable stands arranged between the city wall and Narodni trg, while the

Watch the sun go down and the stars come up while sipping on a cocktail at The Garden

nearby *indoor fish market* on the edge of the harbour is where you can inspect the catch of the day. Haggling is not forbidden! *Daily 6am–3pm*

SUPERNOVA CENTAR ⚑

This shopping centre will set fashionable pulses racing with its selection of international chains from Calzedonia to Zara, alongside a few home-grown Croatian brands. *Daily 9am–9pm | Akcije Maslenica 1*

SPORT & ACTIVITIES

ADVENTURE PARK

This park with mini-golf, zip-wires, water polo and giant trampolines will entertain young and old. *Daily 10am–6pm | on the road to Petrčane | Kožinska cesta 108 | from about 14 euros | adventure-park.hr*

BEACHES

The nearest spot to cool off is *Kolvare* to the south. There are also plenty of pretty, pine-lined beaches to the north of the city on the *Borik* peninsula.

NIGHTLIFE

There is always something happening in the lively ⚑ *Varoš* quarter – for instance at the popular *Caffe Galerija Đina (Varoška 2)* or at *Toni (Mihe Klaića 6)*. If there aren't enough chairs to go round then the pews from *Sv. Mihovil* church are set out on the street.

LEDANA

DJs under the trees at the town's coolest open-air bar in the old town park. It's Zadar's place to party through to the early hours of the morning. *Perivoj kraljice Jelene Madijevke | ledana.hr*

THE GARDEN

Legendary minimalist relaxed bar, featuring international DJs and tasty craft beers. The bar also serves something which is severely lacking elsewhere in Dalmatia: vegan snacks. *Daily 10.30am–1.30am | Bedemi zadarskih pobuna | thegarden.hr/the-garden-lounge*

AROUND ZADAR

1 DAR MAR DONKEY FARM 🐴
10km from Zadar / 15 mins by car
Tractors have largely replaced donkeys out in the fields meaning that they are no longer seen in the olive groves and vineyards. But this farm gives you the chance to stroke these sweet creatures (and even buy their milk). Look for the unmissable donkey statue on the main road to find it. *Poljica 2A | Žerava | tel. 023 390 123 | ⌑ E3*

INSIDER TIP
Dalmatia's animal mascot

2 NIN
13km from Zadar / 15 mins by car
The small town of *Nin* (pop. 1,500) has pre-Roman roots. This island settlement, connected to the mainland by two bridges, used to be a religious centre of the Kingdom of Croatia. The main sights are the *City Gate*, the remains of the *city walls* (15th century) and the *Sv. Križ church*, a superb example of early Christian architecture dating from the ninth century that was used as a coronation venue for seven Croatian kings. Guests at the *Aenona (Ulica Petra Zoranića 2 | tel. 023 265 004 | €)* can sit in the shady garden opposite the church and enjoy the view as they tuck into pizza, fish and grilled dishes.

Nin is especially proud of its "white gold". Salt has been produced in the lagoon landscape surrounding Nin since Roman times, and even today the *Solana Nin* extracts salt using traditional methods and without the aid of additives. There is a small *museum (Mon–Fri 8am–8pm, Sat/Sun 9am–8pm | about 5 euros | Ilirska cesta 7 | solananin.hr)* that explains the 1,500-year history of salt extraction, and tours which take you to salt basins and Roman remains. You can also buy salts, delicacies and cosmetics flavoured with rosemary or lavender from the museum shop. And don't

INSIDER TIP
The perfect blend of sweet and salt

forget to try the *arancini* (orange peel) covered in salty chocolate!

The sandy lagoon surrounding Nin is perfect for surfers. At *Surfmania Surf & Fly Center (mid-April–Oct | Ždrijac| tel. 098 912 9818 | surfmania.hr)* you can hire equipment for surfing and kitesurfing, and sign up for courses to learn the basic techniques. Stand-up paddling is also on offer. The flat sandy *beaches on the Nin Lagoon* are perfect for kids. Don't be surprised if you meet people covered head to toe in black crust at the "Queen's Beach": mud from Nin's sand lagoons has been used for medicinal purposes since Roman times. ⧠ E3

③ ZATON

15km von Zadar / 15 mins by car

The equally historic town of Zaton, just 2km away, is nowadays characterised by beach tourism, and especially for families. *Zaton beach* is flat and sandy and so perfect for kids to build sandcastles and paddle in the cool water – a rarity in Dalmatia. All that remains to remind visitors of Zaton's earlier importance as Nin's trading port is the old Croatian *Sv. Nikolas* church, built on a hill in the 11th century. ⧠ E3

④ PAKLENICA NATIONAL PARK ★

45km from Zadar / 45 mins by car

This national park in the Velebit is a mecca for climbers and walkers. At its heart are two gorges, Mala (small) and Velika (large) Paklenica, carved by streams running through the mountains over thousands of years. *Anića kuk* is a rock formation which attracts pro climbers from all over the world with routes at all levels from 3 to 8b+. Beginners and kids can find simpler routes in the *klanci* section – but don't forget to wear a helmet!

The park is not only a great place to test your physical abilities. Taking a photo safari can help expand your aesthetic horizons.

INSIDER TIP
Natural beauty through a lens

You will be driven through the stunning landscape in a jeep making photo stops along the way and (with a bit of luck) you'll see wild horses too. Great fun for all ages. Among others, *Hotel & Travel Agency Rajna (about 66 euros – for at least 4 people, otherwise 20% more expensive – for a guided day tour including admission, food and drink | Franje Tuđmana 105 | Starigrad-Paklenica | tel. 098 272 878 | hotel-rajna.com/english/fotosafari)* organise great day trips.

Admission June–Sept approx. 9 euros | March, May and Oct approx. 6 euros | Jan and Feb approx. 3 euros | tel. 023 369 155 | np-paklenica.hr | ⧠ E–F3

⑤ PLITVICE LAKES ★

130km from Zadar / 1 hr 45 mins by car

Set among densely wooded mountains there is a valley which seems to belong more to the world of fairy tale than reality. Sixteen glimmering lakes flow into each through a series of

The sun still has to work its wonders before the salt in the lakes at Nin is ready for harvest

waterfalls – it's a landscape that never needs a camera filter. The highest waterfall comes in at 76m and drops into a barely believably blue pool below. This is Croatia's oldest and most famous national park and has UNESCO recognition to prove it. In the summer, it gets very busy. *Spring/ autumn daily 8am–6pm; summer daily 7am–8pm; winter daily 9am–4pm | July and Aug approx. 35 euros until 4pm; approx. 20 euros after 4pm and April, June, Sept and Oct; approx. 7.50 euros Jan, March, Nov and Dec | np-plitvicka-jezera.hr | ▯ F1*

6 IŽ

1.5 hrs from Zadar by catamaran

This island (pop. 600) between Ugljan and Dugi otok is covered in fragrant greenery and olive groves and owes its popularity to the annual folk festival *Iški kralj* (at the end of July/ beginning of August) where an island king is elected. Pottery is a centuries-old tradition in the small town of *Veli Iž*; examples are on display in the *Ethnographical Museum (July and Aug daily 10am–noon, 7–9pm | ⊙ 30 mins). ▯ E3*

7 SILBA

1.5 hrs von Zadar by catamaran, 4 hrs by ferry

Pretty, shingly coves lie alongside the main beach, the sandy *Sotorišće* in the village of Silba, on this 15-km² car-free island (pop. 300). The 30-m "Tower of Love" (Toretta) is an unmissable landmark that was erected by a 17th-century captain so his lover could

UGLJAN & PAŠMAN

Confident swimmers can reach the island of Galovac from Preko's beach

D–E 3–4 **These two sister islands covered with lush foliage are best explored on their beautiful hiking paths, by bike or by spending the day soaking up their tranquillity in remote monasteries and fishing villages.**

The strait separating the two long, narrow islands was only created in 1883, when an isthmus was dug out in order to create a shorter naval route from Zadar to Dugi otok. A bridge was built in the 1970s to connect the islands, which are a popular destination for weekend trips – many people in Zadar own holiday homes here. The accommodation available to holidaymakers generally consists of privately rented rooms and apartments.

PLACES ON UGLJAN

Olive cultivation on *Ugljan* (pop. 7,500, 51km2) dates back to the Roman era, and the olives harvested here in late autumn and winter are used to make one of the best oils in Croatia. A few historic stone houses and an attractive promenade are the highlights of the village of *Preko*, where the ferries from Zadar dock. Alongside the *public lido* on the promenade, a big sandy bay provides great swimming. Close to the ferry port there are also several *konobas*, such as *Konoba Barbara (Put Jerolimovih 4 | tel. 023 286 129 | €€)*, serving fresh

look out for him at sea. Artist Marija Ujević-Galetović's *Sculpture Garden* is well worth a visit.

Silba's other attraction lies underwater in Pocukmarak cove, where archaeologists have unearthed an early Christian sarcophagus and two stone covers used by later generations as material for a jetty. This now serves as an *underwater museum* but there's no need for diving equipment – a mask and flippers will suffice. Accommodation here is only in private rooms or apartments. *D2* grilled fish. An hour's walk uphill leads to the ruins of *Fort Sv. Mihovil* (13th-century), which has a fantastic view over the Zadar archipelago.

Tourists are welcome to visit the Franciscan monastery on the island of *Galovac*, and for less than 1 euro a boat will take you across from the jetty close to the *tourist information centre (Magazin 8)*. The neighbouring villages can easily be explored on bikes. *Nav Travel (Magazin 5 | tel. 023 316 435 | navadriatic.com)* offers bike rental, with a mountain bike costing about 14 euros per day. *Kali*, the next village has a 🐗 snack bar, *Srdela Snack (Zadarska ulica)*, which works with local fishermen to provide its diners with the very freshest grilled sardines and anchovies. One possible destination on your bike ride might be the island's main village of *Ugljan*, around 10km to the north. There, you will find a monastery on a pine-forested peninsula, with a sandy beach and shallow waters. A further 2km to the north and close to *Muline* lies the idyllic, remote sandy beach of Vela Luka. If you're

ER TIP
Paradise sland beach

lucky you might also come across several Roman archaeological sites that are open to the public, but difficult to find.

Travel 8km south from Preko along a road running through pine forests and olive groves to reach *Kukljica*. *Konoba Stari Mlin (tel. 023 373 304 | €€)* serves great food including excellent grilled meat and fish. Around 20 minutes' walk from the village you will find *Sabuša* beach hidden among pine trees on the southwestern coast, with the *Jelenica* nudist bay a few metres further on.

PLACES ON PAŠMAN

Pašman (pop. 3,500, 57km²) is also covered with olive groves and vineyards. An attractive footpath leads you from the main village of *Tkon* up the *Čokovac* hill to the 🐗 *Sv. Kuzma i Damjan monastery (June–Sept Mon–Sat 4–6pm)*. Inside, there is a unique candle holder, which protrudes from the wall in the shape of a human arm.

In *Mrljane*, 8km to the north, the beach is so flat that you need to wade a long way out before the water becomes deep enough to swim in. A bumpy 50-km mountain-bike track circles the island, with plenty of great views along the way. Maps are available from the tourist information centre in Tkon. If you're hungry after all that cycling, sit on the breezy terrace of the restaurant *Lanterna (Pašman | tel. 023 260 179 | lanterna.hr | €€)*, where a large variety of freshly caught fish is served.

DUGI OTOK

📖 *D–E 3–4* **The azure sea, empty beaches and steep cliffs keep people in search of exercise or relaxation coming back to the "Long Island". Its green north is defined by olive groves and copses, but as you travel south down the island's only road, the landscape** constantly changes before finally morphing into the *Telašćica Nature Park* with its karst (limestone) features. Here on the island's southernmost tip, you will get a magnificent view of the sheer and rugged rocky cliffs if you venture out to sea.

Only around 2,400 people live on Dugi otok; its tourist industry is mostly located in the south around the island's main village of *Sali* (pop. 750), and in *Božava* (pop. 160) in the northwest. Mountain bikers will relish the rather steep ⚑ *scenic road* that runs from north to south, with stunning views over the sea and the islands. You can pick up a cycle map from the tourist information centre in Sali, and bikes can be rented from the *Gelateria Conteš (Porat 1 | tel. 098 331 184 | contes.hr)* in Sali *(mountain bike approx. 27 euros/day, branch in Božava)*. Climbers will find routes in *Stara kava*, a disused quarry between the villages of Luka and Savar in the middle of the island.

PLACES ON DUGI OTOK

🟦 BOŽAVA

The houses lining the deep and sheltered cove of *Božava* (pop. 160) couldn't exactly be called picturesque, but the village makes a great base for trips to hidden rocky coves, as well as to the famous sandy beach ⭐ *Sakarun* 3km away. It is also close to the northwestern tip of the island, where the *Veli rat lighthouse* has cast its signal out across the Adriatic since 1849. You can climb the tower's 200 steps if you

ask the lighthouse keeper. *Božava diving school (tel. 023 318 891 | bozava. de/eng)* offers diving trips. Among the few restaurants on the north end of the island, the bistro *Gorgonia (Verunić | tel. 091 737 9823 | gorgonia. hr | also apartments | €€)* is worth the 5km journey from Božava. Here, you can sit on the seafront as you savour freshly cooked fish and meat. *▯▯ D3*

🟦 SALI

This small village (pop. 750) on the southeastern coast welcomes its visitors with a view of pastel-coloured façades clustered round a narrow harbour. There have been fishermen based here for over 1,000 years. The only hotel, *Sali (48 rooms | tel. 023 377*

049 | *hotel-sali.hr* | €€) on Sašćica bay, offers its guests an attractive shingle beach and plenty of sporting activities, while the restaurant *Špageritimo (tel. 023 377 227 | €€€)* has made a name for itself with its creative fish dishes. *E4*

⑩ TELAŠĆICA NATURE PARK

The entrance to this *park (telascica.hr)* is just under 9km to the south of Sali. The park itself comprises the deep, south-facing Telašćica Bay, its 13 rocky islets, and the cliff face where Dugi otok's southwestern coast rises above the Adriatic. Countless boats rest at anchor in the sheltered waters of the bay. An admission charge *(about 6 euros)* is payable at the *office of the park authority*; from this point you will need to walk (or sail) around 2km to the *salt lake Mir*, whose waters are ideal for bathing – and significantly warmer than the sea. There is a spectacular view at the end of the ten-minute climb

INSIDER TIP
Clifftop views

from the nature park office up to the clifftop on the western coast. From the top of *Kliff Grpašćak* there is an almost sheer 160m drop into the sea. From April until October, Goran opens the doors of his *konoba* on the bay, *Go Ro (tel. 098 853 443 | €€€)*. The fish is caught by Goran himself or by his pals, and the vegetables are grown in the garden. *E4*

Dramatic ending: the spectacular cliff face on the southernmost tip of Dugi otok

Telašćica Bay: relax in a hammock after a day at sea

BIOGRAD NA MORU

E4 **Thanks to its role as a point of departure for ferries to Pašman and tours through the Kornati archipelago, this town of 6,000 inhabitants and two marinas is a lively spot during the summer.**

The entire *Biograd Riviera* is full of beautiful beaches and comfortable hotels and campsites, and Biograd na Moru and its neighbours *Sv. Filip i Jakov* and *Pakoštane* are popular resorts. Visitors flock to Biograd for its beautiful coves, pine forests and promenade, but the only sights worth seeing in this town – seat of the Croatian kings in the 11th century – are the museum and the small old town around the 18th-century Sv. Stošije church.

SIGHTSEEING

TOWN MUSEUM 🛆

This museum is well worth a visit on a rainy day: the core of the collection is the cargo of a Venetian ship that sank off Pašman in the 16th century. *Mon–Fri 8am–2pm, 4–8pm, Sat 9am–noon | 1.50 euros | Kralja Petra Krešimira IV 20 | muzej-biograd.com | ⊙ 1 hr*

EATING & DRINKING

CARPYMORE
A favourite on the promenade offering Mediterranean and Italian cuisine. Also B&B *(€€). Kralja Tvrtka 10 | tel. 023 386 119 | carpymore.hr | €€–€€€*

CASA VECCHIA
In this inconspicuous, tree-lined, old town courtyard, you can enjoy the taste of pizza and pasta in the shade. *Kralja Kolomana 30 | tel. 023 383 220 | €€*

FAST FOOD NICO
Nico's toasties and burgers are the best kind of fast food: tasty and good value. He stays open well into the evening too. *Daily 9am–midnight | Trg Kralja Tomislava 6 | €*

SPORT & ACTIVITIES

There are activities of all kinds around here from water parks with large inflatables to parasailing. The diving centre *Albamaris (Dražica beach | albamaris.hr)* takes guests on excursions to the Kornati National Park to dive down to the wreck of a ship and other underwater highlights.

BEACHES

The main beach, *Dražica*, is popular with families thanks to its smooth pebbles, a saltwater pool and waterslides. *Soline* is another shady and sandy beach ideal for children who want to build sandcastles as are the beaches in nearby *Sv. Filip i Jakov.*

Crvena Luka bay to the south is also fringed with sand and is utterly beautiful. You can only get to it from a pricey car park which is often closed when it gets busy.

NIGHTLIFE

Bars line up along the Riva (promenade) serving cocktails. If clubbing is your thing, head to the sandy beach of *Soline*. There are regular concerts by local folk bands or Croatian popstars. Events: *biogradnamoru.hr.*

LAVENDER BED BAR
Relax on comfortable loungers with a cocktail. The bar of the Adriatic Hotel is decorated in purple and is the centre of local nightlife. *Daily until 1am | Tina Ujevića 7*

AROUND BIOGRAD NA MORU

11 KORNATI ARCHIPELAGO ★
The 148 islands and rocky outcrops that make up the *Kornati archipelago* are sprinkled around the sea between Biograd na Moru and the island of Murter. The true beauty of the islands can only be appreciated from the sea (permits to enter the National Park cost upwards of 40 euros per day). Divers flock to the islands every year. On the island of *Ravni Žakan, Konoba Žakan (tel. 091 377 6015 | €€€)* serves

freshly caught fish. If you choose to dine at the *Konoba Levrnaka (tel. 091 435 3777 | €€)* on the island of the same name, you can follow your meal with a dip in crystal-clear waters on the only sandy beach in the whole archipelago. You can also explore the Kornati islands by kayak, on a mountain bike or with a snorkel. *Malik Adventures (tel. 091 784 7547 | malikadventures.com)* organises wonderful kayak tours combined with yoga and bee-keeping classes or dolphin-watching trips.

INSIDER TIP
Paddle in the sun

There are pleasure boats offering trips around the islands from virtually every place on the coast. The cheapest way to get there is to take a ferry, but a smaller boat will be considerably comfier. They normally include lunch and drinks … so long as the seagulls don't steal them from you.

12 FUN PARK BIOGRAD 🎡

5km from Biograd na Moru / 10 mins by car

Wild West, pirates and the universe: Croatia's first theme park opened in 2017 and is waiting for you to test your courage on its rides. If you do manage to get on the roller coaster, you will be rewarded with amazing sea views. Afterwards you can recover in the *Fat Pirate Cave* restaurant. *Summer daily 3–11pm | for unlimited rides: peak season approx. 26 euros, family tickets from 60 euros; it may work out cheaper to pay for rides individually | Jankolovački put 9 | funparkbiograd.com |* ▦ *E4*

13 PAKOŠTANE

6km from Biograd na Moru / 10 mins by car

With the sea on one side and a freshwater lake on the other, the attractive old town of *Pakoštane* (pop. 2,000) is best explored by wandering through its lanes. This will give you the best introduction to this erstwhile fishing village whose pious inhabitants called the three islands just off their coast "Faith", "Hope" and "Love". Pakoštane is a popular bathing spot with families thanks to its gently sloping sandy beaches, such as *Punta* and *Janice*. Windsurfing, kayaking and catamaran trips are offered by *Galeb Adventures (Obala Krešimira 72 | tel. 091 542 3902 | galebaventures.com)*. You can also rent a Zodiac dinghy and explore the Kornati archipelago.

Then you can retreat from the hustle and bustle to the inner courtyard of the *Konoba Pakoštanac (Kraljice Jelene 23 | tel. 023 382 473 | €)* where you'll dine under olive trees on beautifully seasoned grilled meat.

14 VRANA LAKE

10km from Biograd na Moru / 15 mins by car

At *Vransko jezero* you can watch the crows that gave the lake its name (*vrana* = crow) in the reserve at the northern end of the nature park *(admission about 3 euros)*. You are also likely to spot great white egrets and purple herons and, if you're lucky, merlins and marsh harriers. A 40km cycle path runs round the lake (rental at the park authority office in Prosika, about 3 euros per hour) and also passes through the village of *Vrana*, where the ruins of an 11th-century fortress and the Ottoman caravanserai *Maškovica Han (maskovicahan.hr)*, built in 1644–1645, are a reminder of turbulent times. Accommodation, restaurant and a small museum are all available here. The view of the lake, the coastline and the Kornati islands surrounded by the blue of the sea is fantastic from the 250-m-high *Kamenjak* hill. There are picnic benches where you can chow down while taking in the many shades of blue around you. *F4*

INSIDER TIP
Lunch with a view

15 MURTER

40km from Biograd na Moru / 40 mins by car

Most boat trips to the Kornati islands set off from the village of *Murter* (2,000 inhabitants) on the island of the same name. Slanica beach gently slopes down to the sea. Bring your snorkel in order to find a bit of aquatic Roman history: the ruins of the town of *Colentum (Put Gradine)*, some of which are on the beach and some in the shallows around it. After your archaeological research, head to *Zameo ih vjetar (Hrvatskih vladara 5 | tel. 022 434 475 | €€)* to try their special pizza *bubbizza*. *F4*

There's always another island to explore in the Kornati Archipelago

Šibenik's old town with a view of the cathedral

ŠIBENIK

F–G4 **Behind the dreary suburbs of Dalmatia's third-largest port (pop. 47,000) lurks a meandering old town, dotted with Renaissance palaces and brought to life by young musicians. In the summer Šibenik holds back-to-back festivals ranging from jazz *(OFF Jazz & Blues Festival)* to alternative music *(Regius)* and bass *(Membrain)*; so make sure to find out what's on during your stay.**

The UNESCO World Heritage Site of the cathedral *Sv. Jakov* stands on a terrace above the quayside and dominates the city's skyline with its white marble dome. The splendid palaces in the tangle of streets surrounding it and leading up to the ruins of Fort *Sv. Mihovil* (13th–18th centuries) act as a reminder of Šibenik's long history – the city on the Krka estuary was founded by Croatian kings in the 11th century.

Šibenik is an ideal base for touring the nearby *Šibenik archipelago*, with its main islands of *Krapanj* and *Prvić*, and the *Kornati archipelago*. Inland, footpaths and waterways wind between the cascades of the River Krka in the national park of the same name.

SIGHTSEEING

OLD TOWN

The main artery is *Ulica kralja Tomislava*, which has staircases branching off from it. It ends in the *Trg Republike Hrvatske (Square of the Croatian Republic)* with its unique collection of buildings: the *cathedral*, the 16th-century *Loggia* with its wide-arched arcade, and the neighbouring *City Hall (Gradska vijećniva)*. The 15th-century *Rector's Palace (Knežev palač)* was used as a residence by newly appointed dukes at the beginning of Venetian rule, and is today home to the *City Museum (Mon–Fri 8am–8pm, Sat/Sun 10am–8pm | about 4 euros | Gradska vrata 3 | muzej-sibenik.hr | ○ 1 hr)*, which houses a modern exhibition on the history of the city.

The *Dalmatinac Monument* on the square commemorates the architect of the cathedral. The four 15th-century well shafts on the neighbouring *Trg 4 Bunara* mark the spot of an underground cistern which was once used to store water in case of drought or siege. The medieval garden of the 🐗 *St Lovre Franciscan Monastery (Kačićeva 11 | free admission)* is an inviting oasis hidden away in the old town.

On *Ulica kralja Tomislava* look out for small stone troughs which have quenched canine thirst since the 16th century and demonstrate the town's love of animals.

SV. JAKOV CATHEDRAL ★

The city's cathedral is considered to be the masterpiece of architect Juraj Dalmatinac. In 1441 he began work on the existing Gothic structure, adding a transept and a crossing dome to expand it into a bright Renaissance building made exclusively of stone, demonstrating his technical mastery in the process. His skill is particularly evident in the baptistery, whose dome is made up of nine interlocking stone slabs decorated with reliefs. The 74 busts were designed to commemorate prominent citizens and again demonstrate Dalmatinac's eye for detail. His apprentice Nikola Firentinac completed the structure in 1535. *Daily, summer 8.30am–8pm, winter 8.30am–noon, 4–8pm | about 2 euros | ○ 30 mins.*

EATING & DRINKING

In the old town there are lots of bars and cafés.

GRADSKA VIJEĆNICA

The view of the cathedral alone is reason come here for a drink at the very least; but dinner under the Renaissance arcades is charming too, and the food is very good. *Trg Republike Hrvatske 3 | tel. 022 213 605 | €€*

LUCE & BRIGITA

Cheap, cheerful and delicious fish restaurant in the centre. *Uskočka 13 | tel. 091 212 5819 | €*

PELEGRINI

The best restaurant in Dalmatia is not far from the cathedral and boasts a view of the sea. The creative Dalmatian cuisine served here offers an elaborate take on traditional dishes. *Closed Mon | Jurja Dalmatinca 1 | tel. 022 213 701 | €€€*

SHE

An organic restaurant which claims to make food for the soul. Lots of vegan options. *Zlarinski prolaz 2 | tel. 022 215 957 | shebenik.com | €€*

VINO I INO

Wine bar serving a range of cold appetisers and tasty snacks. *Fausta Vrančića | tel. 091 250 6022 | €€*

SHOPPING

GALERIJA JURAJ DALMATINAC

The old stone walls of this gallery are covered in (decent value) art, fashion and jewellery. *Don Krste Stošića 14 | galerijajurajdalmatinac.com*

OGGI BIJOUX

Martina Morić loves colour and combines strips of leather with Swarovski crystals and plastic bracelets with Murano glass in her pieces. Her jewellery is hip and Mediterranean. *Branitelja Domovinskog rata 2d | oggibijoux.com*

SPORT & ACTIVITIES

AQUAPARK 👯

Water park in the Amadria Park resort, 6km outside town. The *kiddy world* will be especially popular with little ones. *Mid-April-Oct daily 9am-8pm (closed in storms) | admission about 15 euros, children measuring 90-120cm about 11 euros | amadriapark.com*

NEXTBIKE ŠIBENIK

Bicycles and e-bikes are the ideal way to get to local beaches and are available all over town. They cost about 1.20 euros per hour to hire. Although you pay a membership fee of about 11 euros when you register by app or online, you get the equivalent free hours on a bike. *nextbike.hr*

BEACHES

Banj is 900m outside the centre of town and has excellent views of the old town. *Rezalište* in Brodarica is, however, the best local beach.

NIGHTLIFE

For concert and festival listings, look online at *sibenik-tourism.hr/en/town-of-festivals*

AZIMUT

This underground venue in a former cistern under Well Square is where the town's alternative scene meets up for concerts, exhibitions and theatre in the vaults. *Mon-Fri 9am-4am, Sat 10am-4am, Sun 9am-1am | Obala palih omladinaca 2*

INSIDER TIP
Concert in a cistern

PUBLIC BAR

This is where Šibenik's young people come together to party and to dance. *Daily until 4am | Bana Josipa Jelačića 2 | FB: publicbarsibenik*

AROUND ŠIBENIK

16 SV. NIKOLA FORTRESS
9km from Šibenik / 15 mins by car

The impressive fort appears to be floating on the sea at the entrance to the St Anthony Channel. Croatia's latest World Heritage Site (2017) was built in the 16th century to protect Šibenik from the open sea. At the time of writing there is extensive restoration work (as well as the construction of a new visitor centre) taking place on the fortress and the land route to it. You can still get to it by boat. Its peaceful atmosphere and photogenic views over Šibenik and Sv. Nikola make it well worth a walk or bike ride along the channel. Your children will love playing on the beach and you can relax in the shade. ⌖ F4

17 VODICE
13km from Šibenik / 18 mins by car

The small town of *Vodice* (pop. 6,700) is one of the most popular resorts on the Dalmatian coast thanks to its shingle beaches – including the famous *Plava plaža* (Blue Beach) – and is also a hotspot for clubbing holidays. The club *Aurora (July–Sept | Kamenar 3 | auroraclub.hr)* stays open all night long and is often played by Croatian stars and DJs. ⌖ F4

18 PRVIĆ
13km from Šibenik / 40 mins by ferry

you need to get away from the crowds, you should visit this car-free island.

Restaurant Pelegrini, Šibenik

The picturesque villages of *Prvić Luka* and *Šepurine* are only a short walk from each other, and between them is an inviting beach. The ☂ *Memorijalni centar Faust Vrančić (Mon–Fri 9am–4pm; July/Aug Mon–Sat 9am–8pm | about 4 euros | Ulica 1a | Prvić Luka)* exhibits more than 50 wooden models built by the first ever inventor to test a parachute – way back in the 16th century. ⌖ F4

The power and beauty of water is on show at the Krka Waterfalls

🔟 KRKA WATERFALLS ★

13km from Šibenik / 20 mins by car
Swimming under these waterfalls in the *Krka National Park* is a magical experience. The River Krka cascades down in the valley here – its high limestone content forming the typical "karst" landscape around you. There are also culturally interesting places here including a monastery isolated on an island in a lake and a Roman amphitheatre. There can be long queues in the summer but they normally move quickly. *Skradin entrance daily 8am–6pm | Roški slap entrance daily 9am–6pm | admission 15–30 euros depending on season | tel. 022 201 777 | npkrka.hr | ▥ G4*

🔟 FALCONRY CENTRE 👥

8km from Šibenik / 15 mins by car
Falconer Emilio Menđušić looks after injured birds before releasing them back into the wild. The team at the falconry centre also conducts research and runs an education programme for local schools. Tourists can get a taste for the place by taking a 45-minute tour which will allow you to see a variety of birds of prey. The centre (Croatian name: *Sokolarski centar*) is on the edge of Dubrava. *Summer daily 9am–7pm | admission about 7 euros, children 6 euros | Škugori | Dubrava kod Šibenika | tel. 091 506 7610 | ⏱ 1.5 hrs | ▥ G4*

22 PRIMOŠTEN

30km from Šibenik / 40 mins by car

Situated on a teardrop-shaped island, the houses of the old town in this picturesque village (pop. 1,500) cluster around the *Sv. Juraj church* (15th century) that sits enthroned on its hill. A causeway connects Primošten to the modern suburbs and hotel complexes on the mainland, while the *Raduča* peninsula with its thick pine forest and 800-m shingle beach lies opposite. Stroll through the town past souvenir shops and cafés until you reach the *parish church* and its peaceful cemetery, which offers a beautiful view of the sea and the mainland. The ★ *vineyards of Primošten* are actually rock-covered slopes with small clearings that offer just enough room for vines to grow. The soil is therefore protected against corrosion from wind and water and the heat stored in the stone by day keeps the grapes warm at night. The result is the *Babić* red wine, which you can sample at the agrotourism restaurant *Baćulov Dvor (Primošten Burnji | baculov-dvor.com | €€)* located 7km to the northeast. Here, you can also try home-grown organic herbs, oil and honey. *⌕ F5*

INSIDER TIP
Rustic yet romantic

21 BRODARICA

11km from Šibenik / 15 mins by car

Despite its many hotels and restaurants, *Brodarica* (pop. 2,500) is still a peaceful resort. The *Zlatna Ribica* restaurant *(Krapanjskih spužvara 46 | tel. 022 350 695 | €€)* is popular for its fish dishes and has wonderful guest rooms as well *(27 rooms, 3 bungalows)*. There is an hourly ferry to the island of *Krapanj*, but you could just swim across to it, as it's only 300m offshore. The island is home to sponge divers, who still perform their dangerous work today. Krapanj is a great diving destination for visitors too. *⌕ F4*

SPLIT REGION

LIVELY CITY WITH MOUNTAIN BACKDROP

The beaches of the Makarska Riviera are unrivalled in Dalmatia, not least because they lie directly beneath the Biokovo mountains. Walkers and climbers can spend their mornings at altitude before diving into the cool sea in the afternoon.

The Roman Emperor Diocletian chose to retire to this richly contrasting coastline and bequeathed to posterity a palace that developed into the bustling city of Split. Croatia's second biggest city

Hvar harbour

has the buzz of a metropolis, with plenty of nightlife but plenty of traditional charm too. Its neighbour Trogir is shaped by its Renaissance buildings.

Makarska's splendid sandy beaches pack the punters in, as do the islands out at sea. One of these – Hvar – has become a party island for the rich and famous, while Brač reels in the windsurfers.

MARCO POLO HIGHLIGHTS

★ **TROGIR**
This whole city is a work of art, from Gothic to Baroque, rounded off with a laid-back Mediterranean lifestyle ➤ p. 68

★ **DIOCLETIAN'S PALACE**
A city giving rise to a palace, or vice versa? Split blends the ancient with the modern ➤ p. 71

★ **SV. DUJE CATHEDRAL**
This Christian church hides a pagan secret: the Emperor's Mausoleum ➤ p. 72

★ **ZLATNI RAT**
This beach or "Golden Cape" is Brač's piece of paradise ➤ p. 78

★ **HVAR TOWN**
A perfect collection of historic buildings with an added dose of liveliness ➤ p. 81

★ **BLUE GROTTO (MODRA ŠPILJA)**
The waters inside this cave on the island of Biševo glow a fairy-tale blue every lunchtime ➤ p. 86

★ **MAKARSKA RIVIERA**
Fifteen resorts scattered along the most beautiful beaches in Central Dalmatia ➤ p. 88

TROGIR

G5 **No city in Dalmatia has such well-preserved Romanesque and Gothic architecture as ★ Trogir (pop. 13,000).**

The elongated island, running between the mainland and the much larger island of Čiovo, is densely populated with churches, palaces and town houses lining narrow streets, while the city's façades and courtyards are full of typical Renaissance architecture. Trogir is no museum, however, as this UNESCO World Heritage Site is brought to life by its residents and holidaymakers. The old town is connected to the modern districts in the north and south by two bridges.

SIGHTSEEING

JOHN PAUL II SQUARE (TRG IVANA PAVLA II)

This square is located at the northeastern end of the historic town. The elegant façade of the 15th-century *Čipiko Palace* opposite *Sv. Lovro Cathedral* is impressive; its Gothic windows were designed by Andrija Aleši, while Nikola Firentinac was responsible for the enchanting inner courtyard. *Gradska ulica*, the main road leading into the square, was briefly named after the German Chancellor Helmut Kohl in the 1990s in thanks for his speedy recognition of an independent Croatia. The eastern end of the square is dominated by the 13th-century *City Hall*, which was renovated during the Renaissance. If the inner courtyard is open you will be able to view its Romanesque staircase and fountain.

SV. LOVRO CATHEDRAL

The harmonically integrated architectural styles of this church – from its Romanesque basement to the Renaissance upper floors – tell the story of its long, 500-year construction from the 13th to the 17th centuries. One masterpiece of the earliest Romanesque phase is the 🐷 *main portal*, which was decorated by Master Radovan with a series of everyday scenes, while Adam and Eve stand on lions around the edge. Inside the church, the *side chapel*, designed by Andrija Aleši, Nikola Firentinac and Ivan Duknović for Bishop John of Trogir, is a bright and flawless Renaissance masterpiece. There's a wonderful view over the old town from the 45m *bell tower*. *Summer Mon– Sat 8am–8pm, Sun noon–6pm' otherwise Mon–Sat 9am–noon | about 3.50 euros | ⏱ 30 mins*

BENEDICTINE MONASTERY (SAMOSTAN SV. NIKOLE)

The monastery museum holds many stunning paintings and church treasures, but they all pale in comparison to the third-century BCE marble relief of Caerus, the Greek god of luck and opportunity. *Summer daily 10am–1pm, 4–5.45pm; if the monastery is closed call: tel. 021 881 631 | about 4 euros | Gradska 2 | ⏱ 30 mins*

KAMERLENGO FORTRESS

Built in the 15th century, this fortress didn't just protect Trogir from attackers,

Sightseeing made easy: all of Trogir's most splendid buildings are on its main square

it also sheltered its resident tax collectors from the wrath of the townsfolk. *July–Sept daily 8am–9pm; May, June and Oct 10am–7pm | about 3.50 euros | in the west of the old town island | 1 hr*

EATING & DRINKING

CALEBOTTA

This stylish bar/restaurant offering fresh Dalmatian cuisine at the heart of the old town leaves nothing to be desired, whether you go for breakfast, lunch or dinner. *Gradska 23 | tel. 021 796 413 | €€*

GROTA

In the neighbouring village of *Seget Donji*, the romantic cave restaurant "Grotto" serves culinary delights and is a popular spot for couples – it would make an ideal setting for a marriage proposal. *Hrvatskih Žrtava 360 | tel. 021 626 498 | €€–€€€*

KONOBA TRS

Tucked away in the courtyard of a 13th-century house in the old town, this upmarket bar serves very special local dishes including lamb *pašticada*, fig ravioli and even lobster *peka* (pre-order). *Matije Gupca 14 | tel. 091 271 0971 | konoba-trs.com | €€–€€€*

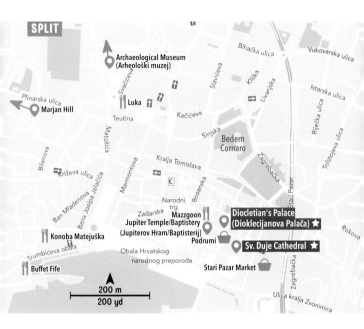

AROUND TROGIR

1 UNDERWATER STATIONS OF THE CROSS

14km from Trogir / 19 mins by car

This is where religious tourism meets outdoor adventures. The world's first underwater Stations of the Cross are in Jelinak bay near Marina, close to Trogir. The 14 stations depicting Jesus on the day of his crucifixion are replicated with 50 life-size sculptures. Beginner divers do not need to fear the 4–9-m depths down to the biblical figures. It's a magical sight when the rays of sunlight fall onto the sculptures through the surface of the water. Underwater lighting means you can go on a pilgrimage dive by night. Contact: *Blue Nautica (Put Cumbrijana 19 | tel. 099 660 0269 | blue-nautica. com).* ⟨⟩ *G5*

2 PANTAN WATERMILL (MLINICE PANTAN)

3km from Trogir / 7 mins by car

The small bird reserve at Pantan is nothing to write home about, unlike the rustic restaurant in a Renaissance mill that is located within the reserve. Part of the floor is tiled with glass so you can see the stream flowing through the mill, and, if you eat in the restaurant, you don't have to pay the entry fee to the conservation area. *Kneza Trpimira 50 | pantan.net | €€ |* ⟨⟩ *G5*

SPLIT

H5 **In the foreground, there's the bustling harbour. Residents and tourists stroll along the flower-bedecked Riva in front of the walls of Diocletian's Palace. Dalmatia's biggest city is like a metropolis on the coast.**

The centre of *Split* (180,000 inhabitants) is shut off from all traffic, noise and crowds. Within the mighty walls of the Roman imperial palace, you will hear nothing but the cooing of pigeons and the church bells. The huge palace district (215m x 180m) was built around 240–312 CE for the Emperor Diocletian, a persecutor of Christians. It formed the basis for the city of Split and today it makes up a part of the old town. Inhabitants of the Roman city of Salona sought refuge in the palace during Slavic attacks in the seventh century. The Roman buildings have withstood 1,500 years of habitation extraordinarily well and, in 1979, the palace was declared a UNESCO World Heritage Site. ➤ The *Split Card (about 10 euros, valid for 72 hrs | short. travel/kkd12)* gets you discounts or free admission at lots of sights.

SIGHTSEEING

DIOCLETIAN'S PALACE ★
From the Riva, visitors enter this ancient complex through its basement, the *Podrumi (June–Sept daily 8.30am–9pm; Oct–May shorter; closed Sun afternoon | about 6 euros)*. The high ceiling is supported on brick

WHERE TO START?

The best starting point for a sightseeing tour is the waterfront promenade **Obala Hrvatskog narodnog preporoda** – or **Riva** for short – in front of Diocletian's Palace. There is a car park here, but it is often full (there's an alternative on Vukovarska ulica). To the west of the palace is the old town around the lively **Narodni trg**.

arches and walls that divide the basement up into 50 rooms using exactly the same floor plan as the imperial apartments above. From here, a staircase takes you up to the open air, where you will find a *peristyle* surrounded by arcades with Corinthian columns. A further staircase leads to the *vestibule*, the only room still preserved today, which offers a good overview of the rest of the ancient structure. On the right, the emperor's mausoleum was converted into *Sv. Duje Cathedral*, which rises from the peristyle, while the *baptistery*, a former *Temple of Jupiter*, is diagonally opposite. The *cardo* and *decumanus* – the two main streets crossing at right angles to each other in any Roman town – are today known as *Ulica Dioklecijanova* and *Krešimirova*, and lead to the city gates of the *Porta Ferrea* (Iron Gate) in the west, the *Porta Argentea* (Silver Gate) in the east, and the main *Porta Aurea* (Golden Gate) in the north.

SV. DUJE CATHEDRAL ★

At the heart of the cathedral is the octagonal mausoleum of the Roman Emperor Diocletian, whose ornamented Corinthian columns now frame one of Dalmatia's most beautiful altars. Juraj Dalmatinac created this touching relief of the Flagellation of Christ in 1422. Also noteworthy are the richly decorated Roman portal and the treasury containing the relics of St Domnius *(2 euros)*. Visitors with a head for heights should climb the 60m *bell tower* to enjoy the glorious views. *Mon–Sat 8.30am–7pm, Sun 12.30–6.30pm | joint ticket bell tower, treasury and baptistery about 6 euros | ⏱ 1 hr*

TEMPLE OF JUPITER/BAPTISTERY (JUPITEROV HRAM/ BAPTISTERIJ)

The tiny fifth-century temple (in the palace to the west of the peristyle) was converted into a Christian baptistery in the seventh century, and is guarded by a stone sphinx. Its cruciform baptismal font is decorated with ancient Croatian relief sculpture. *In summer daily 8.30am–7.30pm | 1.50 euros | ⏱ 1 hr*

ARCHAEOLOGICAL MUSEUM (ARHEOLOŠKI MUZEJ)

If you are not planning to visit the Salona archaeological site then make sure you go to Croatia's oldest archaeological museum (founded in 1820). It documents the history of the Romans in Dalmatia with the help of mosaics and other artefacts. *June–Sept Mon–Sat 9am–2pm, 4–8pm; Oct–May Tue–Fri 9am–2pm, 4–8pm, Sat 9am–2pm | 4 euros | Zrinsko-Frankopanska 25 | ⏱ 1 hr*

MARJAN HILL

To the west of the harbour the 3.5-km² Marjan peninsula is covered in thick and shady greenery. This is where residents of Split come to jog, cycle or swim. Nestled among the trees you will find chapels and churches dating from the 16th and 17th centuries. There is also a beautiful 16th-century Jewish cemetery which stands as a memorial to the Spanish persecution of Jews during the Reformation. A 378-step staircase built in 1924 takes you to the highest point (178m). After a stroll, take a break in the *Café Vidilica (Nazorov prilaz 1)*. The peninsula is also surrounded by pebbly beaches such as *Bene, Ježinac* and *Kašjuni*.

> **INSIDER TIP**
> **Memorial in a conservation area**

Ivan Meštrović (1883–1962), Croatia's most renowned sculptor, is mainly known for his monumental sculptures. His summer residence, now the ☂ *Galerija Meštrović*, shows the diversity and intricacy of his works. *May–Sept Tue–Sun 9am–7pm; otherwise Tue–Sat 9am–4pm, Sun 10am–3pm | about 6 euros | Šetalište Ivana Meštrovića 46 | mestrovic.hr*

EATING & DRINKING

BUFFET FIFE

This harbour bar is simple and jolly; the food is tasty home-cooked fare that comes in huge portions. Among the people of Split the deep-fried little fish are a firm favourite. *Trumbićeva obala 11 | tel. 021 345 223 | €*

KONOBA MATEJUŠKA
You have to reserve at this tiny restaurant but it serves by far the best local cuisine around, with plenty of fish. *Tomića Stine 3 | tel. 021 321 086 | villamatejuska.hr | €€€*

LUKA
It's definitely worth queuing for what is easily the best ice cream in the city. It's home-made and comes in a variety of interesting flavours all made from natural ingredients. *Svačićeva 2 | FB: LukaIceCream*

MAZZGOON
Right next to the walls of Diocletian's Palace, this great fun restaurant boasts of its "mostly friendly" staff. Thankfully the food is always delicious and offers modern takes on local classics. *Bajamontijeva 1 | tel. 098 987 7780 | mazzgoonfood.com | €€–€€€*

VEGGIE OPTIONS
Tasty alternatives for vegetarians and vegans are available at *Makrovega (Leština 2 | makrovega.hr | tel. 021 394 440 | €€)*, who serve creative dishes, *Vege Fast Food (Put Porta 2 | €)* for cheap snacks, or the sophisticated *Up Café (Domovinskog rata 29a | upcafe.hr | €€)*.

The belltower of St Domnius' Cathedral overlooks Diocletian's Palace

A shopping stroll in the Palace cellar

clothing made from sustainable and fair-trade materials. *The ID Concept Store (Bana Jelačića 3)* offers an eclectic mix of clothing from Croatian and international designers. If you want to pick up some unique jewellery head to *Break Time Croatia (Trogirska 8 | nautical-bracelets.com)* who make beautiful, nautically themed bracelets – which can be engraved on request.

INSIDER TIP
Seaside fashion

PODRUMI

Parts of the subterranean vaults of Diocletian's Palace are filled with market stands selling souvenirs, books, handmade jewellery and beautiful replicas of Roman mosaics.

STARI PAZAR MARKET

A fruit and vegetable market next to Diocletian's Palace. Also sells souvenirs. Daily.

SPORT & ACTIVITIES

MOUNT MARJAN

Get active on the city's local Mount Marjan! Climb its steep southern slopes or take a mountain bike down its many trails. Bike hire on the Riva: *Baracuda (Trumbiceva ob. 13 | baracuda.com.hr)*; *Split Rent Agency (Obala Lazareta 3 | split-rent.com)*.

PINELI & VINO

A taste of the artist's life. A painting lesson lubricated by a wine tasting is sure to help you discover your creative side. If you stay sober long enough, you'll have a lovely souvenir to take

SHOPPING

FASHION

Creations from Croatian designers hang from the clothes racks at the *Think Pink (Zadarska 8 and Marulićeva 1)* boutique. The friendly *Krug Store (Nepotova 1 | krugstore.com)* in the old town specialises in natural chic

home too. *30 euros per person incl. materials and wine | Jerina 1 | tel. 099 688 6359 | artbottega.com.hr*

SEMI SUBMARINES 👪

Seeing schools of fish swimming by the portholes on these bright red semi-subs is always a great hit with kids. The view from the deck isn't bad either. *Daily 10am–11pm | about 15 euros | jetty in the middle of the Riva | semisubmarine-split.com*

BEACHES

Split's city beach *Bačvice* (shingle and concrete) is southeast of the old town. Residents come here not just to bathe, but also to play the locally invented sport of *picigin*. The players stand in ankle-deep water and try to keep a tennis ball in the air for as long as possible. It does not sound too tricky but you don't score points as you do in volleyball; instead, players are given marks for creative play – a bit like figure skating in the shallows! Other beaches can be found on the Marjan peninsula and in the coves to the south, such as the popular *Obojena svjetlost* in *Kaštelet*.

INSIDER TIP
Real beach volleyball

NIGHTLIFE

In this young city of students, there are a lot of clubs and bars to choose from. Start your evening with an aperitif at the *Café Vidilica (Nazorov prilaz 1)* with its view over the Adriatic islands, or at *Getto (Dosud 10)*, where you can sink into deep armchairs amid flowers and water fountains. The combination of jazz and old books creates a special ambience at the *Marvlvs Library Jazz Club (Papalićeva 4)*. Later in the evening, Split's hip young crowd congregate at *Vanilla (Poljudski put)*, at the exclusive *Hemingway (Mediteranskih igara 5)* or at one of the clubs around Bačvice beach.

However, to see why Split is considered the cultural capital of the region, you need to come between July and September for the city's cultural festival *Evo Ruke (from 9pm | revija-urbane-kulture.com)*. Every night there are concerts from every genre imaginable in the central *Strossmayera (aka Đardin)*. And it is completely free!

AROUND SPLIT

⓷ KAŠTELA (ROUTE OF THE CASTLES)
12–21km from Split / 20–30 mins by car

The so-called "Route of the Castles" connects seven castles from the 15th and 16th centuries, situated on the bay west of Split: *Sućurac, Gomilica, Kambelovac, Lukšić, Stari, Novi* and *Štafilić*.

Under Habsburg rule this section of the coast became the Split Riviera, as testified by its many historic villas and grand hotels (most of which are now rather dilapidated). Socialist

Yugoslavia transformed it into a base for heavy industry and, as a result, the modern Kaštela is something of a mishmash, with wonderful parks and a few restored castles rubbing shoulders with rusting industrial complexes. Perched impressively on a rocky island, *Kaštel Gomilica* is worth a visit.

The biblical garden *Biblijski vrt (Put Gospe Stomorije bb | free admission)* in *Stomorija* offers a tranquil paradise surrounded by plants and biblical sculptures. ⧉ *G-H5*

4 ŠKOPLJANCI RECREATED VILLAGE

35km from Split / 50 mins by car

The traditional Croatian way of living is creatively brought to life in this restored village with refurbished stone houses, hearty food in authentic *konobas* and folk performances. This nostalgic trendsetter has kicked off something of a fashion for restored villages showing off local traditions elsewhere. *Radošić | tel. 021 805 777 | adosic.com | ⧉ G5*

5 KLIS

14km from Split / 30 mins by car

This imposing fortress, once known as the "Key to Dalmatia", towers above the town of the same name to the north of Split. Its strategic position meant that it was used by Roman, Croatian, Venetian and Ottoman emperors – and even by rulers with dragons: Klis is one of the filming locations for *Game of Thrones*. Although you won't see the approach of enemy troops from the watchtowers today, you will be treated to amazing views over the coastal landscape. The railings around the towers are precariously low to say the least and definitely not suitable for small children. *Daily 9.30am–4pm | admission 6 euros | tvrdavaklis.com | ⧗ 2.5 hrs |* ⧉ *H5*

6 ŠOLTA

30 mins from Split (Catamaran) / 1 hr by ferry

This island (58km2, pop. 1,700) lies just off the coast by Split and has a wonderfully rural feel, despite its proximity to the city. Its olive groves produce one of the best oils in Croatia, and accommodation is available almost exclusively in private rooms and apartments. The very intense local wine, Dobričić, is best sampled at the *Purtića*

INSIDER TIP
Red wine unique to the island

dvor vineyard *(Thu-Tue 10am–1pm, Wed 6–9pm | Put crikve 19, Srednje selo | tel. 098 385 425)*, which is run by Mirjana and Tomislav Purtić.

The island's tourist centres are *Nečujam* and *Stomorska* in the east. There are good bathing spots along the northern coast; the rocky south coast is only accessible from the sea. ⧉ *G5*

BRAČ

⧉ *H-J 5–6* **La dolce vita on idyllic beaches meets traditional agriculture inland: the small island of Brač is full of contrasts.**

The beach of Zlatni rat, the "Golden Cape", on the island of Brač

Brač's most famous beach *Zlatni rat*, or the "Golden Cape" is a sickle of fine shingle that sometimes points to the east, sometimes to the west, depending on the currents. However, it would be a shame to focus exclusively on this idyllic spit and ignore the rest of what is the largest island in Central Dalmatia (395km2, approx. 15,000 inhabitants). Bare, scrub-covered surfaces are as much a part of the landscape here as the irrigated and cultivated valley slopes planted with olive and fig trees or vines. Brač is blessed with a precious building material – brilliant white limestone, which is known as "Brač marble" – that has been quarried since Roman times. It has two major advantages: it is relatively soft and therefore easy to "harvest", as the people of Brač say, and it is equally easy to work. It also hardens and becomes stronger over time. The stone is still quarried today in a few places on the island.

PLACES ON BRAČ

7 SUPETAR

The town (pop. 3,200) of Sv.Petar (St Peter) on the north coast is Brač's second-largest resort as well as a port for car ferries from the mainland. The old town is dominated by the *Church of St Mary Annunciation* with its impressive Baroque staircase. On the ground outside the church, you will find a sixth-century Christian

INSIDER TIP
Trample over history

mosaic which shows where St Petrus Basilica once stood.

A 15-minute walk along the beach will take you to the picturesque cemetery at the tip of the Sv. Nikola peninsula. The beaches to the west of the spit Bili rat offer a good alternative to the crowded main beach; here, you will find coves bordered by shady pine forests. The majority of the large beach hotels gather around Vela Luka bay to the west. Further afield, you will also find good (sun)bathing spots in the smaller and larger bays.

At the *Konoba Luš (daily from 5pm | Put Viščica 55 | tel. 099 803 3646 | €€)* you can dine in the attractive setting of an olive grove. You can reach many other beaches and attractive villages by bike; visit *Freni Opačak (Vlačica bb | tel. 095 521 7611 | rent-a-bike-brac. com)* for well-maintained bicycles and route advice.

A few kilometres to the east is the peaceful village of *Splitska*, set perfectly on the slopes of a deep cove. The picturesque village of *Mirca*, 4km to the west, is also worth a visit. At the *Muzej uljarstva (tel. 021 630 900)* you can learn how olive oil is pressed (advance booking required) and the oil is available to purchase.

8 PUČIŠĆA

It is easy to see that this town (pop. 1,700), situated in a deep and narrow cove on the island's north coast, is a centre for Brač's characteristic stone. With its bright houses arranged around the harbour, its souvenir stands selling bowls and figurines carved from white limestone, and its attractive *Renaissance Church of the Assumption* with tombs carved by stonemasons from the island, Pučišća comes across as a very authentic place.

There are lots of narrow strips of beach around to bathe from as well as the glorious *Uvala Luke* around 3km to the east. Here, five coves connect in an inlet of the sea. In Luke cove *Taverna Pipo (tel. 021 784 5495 | pipo1.com | €€€)* serves freshly caught fish. In Pučišća itself, the bistro *Fontana (Trg B. Deskovića 4 | tel. 021 633 515 | €€)* serves simple dishes and is very popular. ⌼ *H5*

9 BOL

The village of *Bol* (pop. 1,600) sprawls along the south coast at the foot of the island's highest mountain, *Vidova gora* (778m). Bol's popularity as a seaside resort is due to its very long fine-shingle beach ★ 🌴 *Zlatni rat (Golden Cape)* and the village's mild climate, as the mountain shelters it from the cold northeasterly Bora wind. However, in the middle of summer, you might feel as if you're in a tin of sardines at this beautiful spot.

The picturesque centre of Bol is a maze of small streets clustered around the harbour and lined with traditional stone houses. The village has lots of guesthouses, souvenir shops and restaurants, but there is also a niche for modern art: the *Galerija Dešković (June–Sept Tue–Sun 9am–noon, 6–11pm, Oct–May Tue–Sat 9am–3pm | 2 euros)* exhibits works by contemporary Croatian artists in a Baroque palace by the harbour.

IDER TIP
**elebration of
tubbornness**

The "House in a House" on Donja obala, which can only be viewed from outside, is one of the weirder local attractions. In the 19th century, the wealthy Vuković brothers chose this spot to build a family palace. The only problem was that there was already a house there and the owner did not want to give it up. In a fit of stubbornness the brothers began to build their house around his. They then died in a storm and the old house survived.

A short walk to the east will bring you to the *Dominican monastery (June-Oct daily 10am-noon, 4-7pm | 2 euros | Anđelka Rabadana 4),* whose museum displays prehistoric artefacts and a painting by Tintoretto, among other items. The monastery's gardens and the nearby shingle beach at Martinica are also well worth a visit.

The reliably consistent Maestral wind makes Bol one of Dalmatia's windsurfing centres (alongside Orebić). You can also hire mountain bikes and kayaks from *Big Blue Sport (Podan Glavice 2 | bigbluesport.com)* on Borak beach.

An old mill forms the centrepiece of the comfortable *Konoba Mlin (Ante Starčevića 11 | tel. 021 635 376 | €€),* which makes an excellent *pašticada.* Slightly higher up the hill above all the hustle and bustle lies the restaurant *Ranč (Hrvatskih domobrana 6 | tel. 021 635 635 | €-€€),* which serves mostly rustic grilled dishes and traditional Dalmatian cuisine. In the evening, partygoers congregate at *Varadero (Frane Radića 1).* And at the

Owners anchor their boats in Supetar's port while they enjoy the nightlife

The 16th-century Blaca hermitage is a popular destination for hikers

end of July, Bol becomes a surprising home for a hip hop and graffiti festival, the *Graffiti na gradele (graffitina gradele.tumblr.com).*

10 BLACA MONASTERY (PUSTINJA BLACA)

A boat takes tourists from Bol into the 'desert' – but one without camels or sand. The *monastery (Pustinja Blaca)* was named 'desert' *(pustinja)* because it was founded in a remote valley by monks fleeing the Ottomans in the 16th century *(walk from the quay: 45 mins | about 16 euros).* The monastery is one of the last places to still use the old Croatian ecclesiastical alphabet, *glagolica.* There is also a small *museum (Tue–Sun 9am–5pm | about 6 euros).* ▢ H6

11 MURVICA

There is a hermitage 6km west of Bol. The *Dragon's Cave (Zmajeva špilja)* was home to hermits from the 15th century and it takes its name from a relief sculpture carved into the rock by early Christians. You have to register at the tourist information centre in Bol before you visit. ▢ H6

12 INLAND VILLAGES

The houses in the shepherd village of *Gornji Humac,* 10km to the north of Bol, are built out of undressed stone with roofs made of stone slabs as protection from the powerful winds up on the plateau (485m). The rustic *Konoba Tomić (tel. 021 647 228 | €)* also rents accommodation *(9 rooms)* while the restaurant serves organically grown meat and vegetables.

The village of *Škrip*, 20km further northwest, is the oldest settlement on the island and is believed to have been inhabited since 1400 BCE. Its centre is wonderfully preserved with defensive walls, a church and a tower. The *Muzej otoka Brača (daily in summer 8am–8pm | 2 euros)* in the 16th-century *Radojković Tower* explains the history of the village, and reminders of Roman times are provided by a relief of Hercules, as well as a mausoleum.

Brač's white stone has also been a source of inspiration to artists, and a regular clan of sculptors lives and works in *Donji Humac* (3km east of Škrip, 20km northwest of Bol). Great-grandfather Jakšić opened the workshop in 1903, and the youngest Jakšić is the sculptor Lovre junior, whose works transform stone into a seemingly fluid material. The family welcomes visitors to their 🐷 *Galerija Jakšić (no fixed opening times | tel. 021 647 710 | drazen-jaksic.hr).* | 🕮 *H5–6*

HVAR

🕮 *G–J6* **Although this "Croatian Ibiza" has become the trendy island, away from the celebrities flocking to its capital you can still find down-to-earth *konobas* and unspoilt beach coves.**

Hvar (pop. 11,000) measures just under 300km^2 and is Croatia's most cosmopolitan island hence its popularity with VIPS. In summer, the purple lavender blossom casts clouds of fragrance over the island. The most beautiful beaches are found on the neighbouring *Pakleni otoci*, the "hell islands", which can be reached by taxi boat (approx. 6 euros per person). The name doesn't really fit this swimming and snorkelling paradise and in fact it's not *pakleni* (hell), but *paklina* (tar, used to weatherproof ships) that the islands are named after. On a guided kayak tour with *Hvar Adventure (Jurja Matijevića 20 | 4 hrs incl. snack and wine about 50 euros | tel. 021 717 813 | hvar-adventure.com)* participants paddle from cove to cove while the sun sets on the horizon. Hiring an electric bike in order to explore the mountainous island of Hvar on two wheels is great fun. Well-maintained bikes can be hired from *e-bike Croatia (bike from 25 euros/day | Ive Roic 6 | tel. 091 584 9841 | e-bike-croatia. com)* in Hvar.

PLACES ON HVAR

🔟 HVAR TOWN ⭐

During the summer, an armada of luxury yachts bob at their moorings along the promenade, the Riva, while their wealthy owners party in the clubs and restaurants of the town (pop. 4,200). Hvar is trying to shake off its party image by implementing draconian measures, for example to those caught sightseeing in beachwear.

Fortunately, most of these VIPs pay little attention to Hvar's real attractions, so you can still take a relaxed stroll through the old town. The *Trg Sv. Stjepana*, the main square, is a feast for the eyes. The bakery *Slastičarna Hvar* makes lavender ice cream. It often produces a Marmite reception: you'll either love it or hate it, so give it a try. The square links the harbour (*mandrač*) and *Sv. Stjepan*'s cathedral. The latter's Renaissance façade and elegant tower are stunning. Another striking building is the 16th-century *Arsenal*, which was used to conceal Venetian warships from prying eyes and to store grain.

In what used to be the aristocratic quarter of *Groda* – which runs from the *Pjaca* almost all the way up the hill to the fortress – you will find the Baroque Benedictine Convent *Samostan Benediktinki (June–Sept Mon–Fri 10am–noon, 5–7pm | about 1.50 euros)*, where the nuns make delicate doilies from agave fibres. The most beautiful examples of their work are on display in the small museum. From the 🐷 *Španjola fortress (summer, daily 8am–midnight; spring/autumn 9am–9pm | about 6 euros)* you can look out over the old town and the neighbouring *Pakleni otoci* archipelago and also explore an exhibition of archaeological artefacts.

Peace and quiet can be found at the Franciscan convent *Franjevački samostan (Mon–Sat 9am–3pm, 5–7pm | 5 euros | Put križa)*, situated to the south of the centre. This 15th-century convent contains a *museum* displaying discoveries from below the sea, as well as a stunning cloister. You won't want to leave the neighbouring garden with its 300-year-old cypresses.

Hrvoje Tomičić offers sophisticated cuisine at *Kod Kapetana (Fabrika 30 | tel. 021 742 230 | €€€)*: everything here is freshly prepared, from lobster to lamb, all with a view of the old town.

🐷 If you want a budget snack at the water's edge, you can't do much better than the wraps and sandwiches sold by *Pakleni otoci*. A bit off the main drag (near the Franciscan monastery) Đorđota Vartal runs the excellent *Restoran Vartal (Fulgencija Careva 1 | tel. 021 743 077 | restoran-vartal.com | €€)*, which specialises in meat dishes.

Evenings in Hvar typically begin with a *korzo* – an evening stroll on the main square. The stylish *Carpe Diem* on the promenade is a popular place to have a drink, but for a more relaxed atmosphere visit the bar *Zimmer Frei (Gornja cesta)* in a back street of the old town. A little further on you will find Ka' Lavanda Music Bar *(Mate Miličića 7 | kalavanda.com)*. Lola Bar *(Sveti Marak 8 | €€)* serves delicious cocktails and burgers alongside great music – try the RunLolaRun cocktail! *Carpe Diem* offers a private shuttle service to its *Carpe Diem Beach (May–Sept daily 8am–8pm, longer at events | carpe-diem-hvar.com)* in *Stipanska Bay* on the island of *Marinkovac*, where sun worshippers will find entertainment in the form of a restaurant, lounge bar and DJ sets.

The village of *Brusje*, a lavender-farming centre situated 6km to the northeast of Hvar town, is easy to cycle to. Lavender products, including aromatic lavender honey, are sold almost everywhere here. For organic food such as olive oil, cheese or wine,

The main square, Pjaca, in Hvar resembles a VIP lounge in summer

visit the *Green House Hvar (Kroz Burak 27)*. ⬜ *H6*

🏠 STARI GRAD

8km from Hvar / 12 mins by car

A pleasant counterpoint to Hvar is the town of Stari Grad (pop. 2,400), whose relaxed Mediterranean vibes attract its own class of visitor. This settlement on a deep and narrow cove in the north of the island was originally founded by Greek colonists in the fourth century BCE. Stari Grad was once an important cultural centre. The Croatian Renaissance poet Petar Hektorović (1487–1572) hosted the brightest minds of his time for discussions at his fortress-like *Villa Tvrdalj (May–Oct daily 10am–1pm, 5.30–8.30pm | 2 euros)*. The grounds include a fishpond set in an arcaded courtyard, whose walls are decorated with Latin aphorisms that offer an insight into the philosophical world of the poet. Hektorović and his daughter Lucrezia are depicted in a portrait in the church of the *Dominican monastery*, which was painted by none other than Tintoretto. You can also inspect the remains of the ancient city walls close to the *Sv. Ivan church*.

The *Stari Grad Plain* – a fertile karst valley running from Stari Grad to Jelsa – is a UNESCO World Heritage Site, as its wine and olive plantations are still arranged in the pattern set out by Greek colonists in the fourth century BCE. The stone walls bordering these fields and the huts used by the farmers are also based on ancient designs.

Head to *Konoba Zvijezda mora (Trg Petra Zoranića | tel. 099 299 1603 | zvijezdamora.com | €€€)* for a great dinner expertly made by Tomislav Subašić using regional products and herbs. In the hamlet of *Dol*, 4km to the east, the *Konoba Kokot (from 6pm | Kuničića dvor 8 | Dol St Ana | tel. 091 511 4288 | €)* serves organic regional cuisine; you'll find all kinds of goat's cheese as well as kid meat on the menu. ⬚ *H6*

⓯ VRBOSKA, JELSA & SURROUNDINGS

The two harbour towns of *Vrboska* and *Jelsa* are located on the island's north coast, to the east of Stari Grad, and are notable for their unique settings on deep, sheltered bays. Vrboska's relaxed atmosphere and the shingle coves on the *Glavica* peninsula attract plenty of day-trippers during the summer. Aside from the narrow harbour with its ancient stone bridge, the town's main sight is the 16th-century fortified church of *Sv. Marija (daily in summer 10am–noon, 7.30–9pm | 2 euros)*, which sits on a hill above the town. *Gardelin (Vrboska bb. | tel. 021 774 280 | €€)* serves excellent food in the marina. To try something local, order *gregada*, a fish stew.

INSIDER TIP
Fisherman's food

Jelsa is more touristy and has lots of campsites. Visit the *Konoba Dvor Duboković (from 6pm | tel. 098 172 1726 | dvordubokovic.hr | €€)* in the village of Pitve, 2km away, for some hearty Dalmatian fare. Make sure you try the home-made sour cherry and

All kinds of seafood and fish are cooked together in the Hvar fish stew known as *gregada*

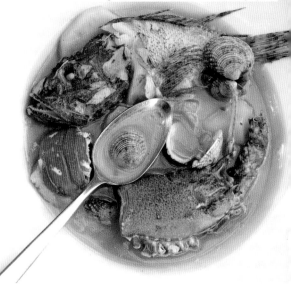

rose liqueurs! Visitors with an interest in winemaking should make the trip from Pitve to Zavala (approx. 5km) and continue a further 7km west along the coast until they reach *Sv. Nedjelja*. Here, you can judge the effects of the special climate and soil for yourself in the *Konoba Bilo Idro (tel. 021 745 709 | €€€)*. The vintner Zlatan Plenković produces the best wines on the island, including the famous *Zlatan otok*. You can also dine on fresh fish, or a platter of *pršut* (prosciutto) and cheese.

The model village of *Humac (free admission)*, 7km east of Jelsa, was once populated by shepherds. Their 17th-century stone houses have been carefully restored and you can even spend the night in one of the rooms. Another appealing option is the traditional *Konoba Humac (tel. 091 523 9463 | reservation advisable | FB: Konoba-Humac-357534557644483 | €€)* which offers tours to the *Caves of Grapčevo* further south. ▯ H6

VIS

▯ G6 **The ferry trip from Split to the remote island of Vis (pop. 3,500) takes around two hours; this remoteness may explain why Vis remains one of the few islands relatively undiscovered by tourists, for it is not short of idyllic beaches and secluded coves.**

It was settled in the fourth century BCE by ancient Greeks (who called it *Issa*), followed by Romans and Slavs. Vis then came under Venetian rule during the 15th century. After the Venetians left, the Habsburgs took over for more than a century, before Tito arrived in 1943 and set up a command centre. During the socialist era Vis became a naval base and access was restricted; only in 1992 did the 91-km^2 island open its doors to tourists. The former military building and underground tunnel of the "forbidden island" can be

INSIDER TIP
Tito's hidden island

explored on a *Military Tour (bookable through the travel agency Vis Special | vis-special.com | 4-hr tour approx. 55 euros)*. Visitors will find fertile landscapes, a rugged coast dotted with coves, and the two small towns of *Komiža* and *Vis*. The first Discovery Tour (see p. 120) will help you explore the island on two wheels.

PLACES ON VIS

The island's main town (pop. 1,900) lies on a horseshoe-shaped cove on the northeastern coast. Traces of ancient Issa are already apparent from the sea on your way into the harbour. On the tip of the spit there is a 🐎 *Greek necropolis* and a little further down you will find the foundations of a *Roman bath* (freely accessible). The *Archaeological Museum (June–Sept Mon–Fri 10am–1pm, 5–8pm, Sat 10am–1pm | about 3 euros | Šetalište viški boj 12)*, in the former Habsburg harbour fort *(Baterija della Madonna)*, displays beautiful amphorae, statues and everyday objects. The cosy *Konoba Kod Paveta (Ivana Farolfija 42 | tel. 021*

711 344 | €€) may only have a small terrace but the delicious traditional food makes up for it.

The experts at *ANMA Diving (Apolonia Zanelle 2 | tel. 091 521 3944 | anma.hr)* will take you to the best diving spots.

🔟 KOMIŽA

Stone houses line the natural harbour, where fishermen used to weigh anchor to go in search of sardines. Today, this quiet town (pop. 1,200) is a popular sailing destination. At the *Fishermen's Museum Ribarski muzej (daily 10am–noon, 8–11pm | about 3 euros)* in the Venetian *watchtower* you can see a replica *falkuša* – a traditional fishing boat. Two shingle beaches, *Gusarica* and *Kamenica*, invite you to take a dip in the sea. Fish, lobster and seafood set the (pricey) tone in the *Konoba Jastožera (Gundulićeva 6 | tel. 021 713 859 | €€€)*,

INSIDER TIP
Pizzas at a good price

while *Karijola (Šetalište viškog boja 4 | tel. 021 711 358 | €€€)* serves delicious wood-fired pizzas at a fair price and with the added bonus of a fabulous view of the promenade. 🕮 G6

AROUND VIS

🔢 BLUE GROTTO (MODRA ŠPILJA) ★

From Vis around 1 hr 15 mins, from Komiža 30 mins by boat

If you want to take a trip to the neighbouring island of *Biševo* to see its famous *Blue Grotto (Modra špilja)* you should enlist the help of an agency to take you from Komiža to the cave at the right time of day. Sunlight causes the water in the cave to glow a radiant turquoise colour, but only for a short time around midday *(numerous agencies in Komiža, admission about 9.50 euros).* 🕮 G7

OMIŠ

🕮 H5 **This town (pop. 16,000) at the entrance to the Cetina Gorge was a notorious pirates' lair in the Middle Ages, a proverbial thorn in the side for local rulers.**

From the 11th century, Slavic pirates used its sheltered location as a base for rapid raids; it wasn't until 1444 that Venice managed to conquer Omiš. Two fortresses, *Fortica* and *Mirabella (entry about 3 euros each)* high up on the cliff watch over the old town's quiet streets and bear witness to this history of conflict with the Ottomans.

EATING & DRINKING

KONOBA MILO

Among the many restaurants here, Milo stands out with its personal service and delicious Dalmatian cuisine. *Knezova Kačića 15 | tel. 021 861 185 | €€*

SPORT & ACTIVITIES

Traditional festivals keep Omiš's rich history alive. In July there is a

Hold on tight and enjoy the views from the zipline over the Cetina Gorge

competition for the best *klapa* choir in Croatia *(Festival dalmatinskih klapa)*, while mid-August *Pirate Night (Gusarska noć)* re-enacts a spectacular 13th-century sea battle between the Venetians and local pirates. 👯 During the day there are pirate games for children.

For a dose of adrenalin try the zipline, where you hang from a cable 150m up and shoot across the canyon at speeds of up to 65km per hour. *Agencija Malik (approx. 55 euros | Josipa Pupačića 4 | tel. 095 822 2221 | zipline-croatia.com)*.

BEACHES

There are good beaches on both sides of the Cetina estuary including some with gloriously soft sand such as *Velika plaža*, popular with volleyball players and para-sailors.

NIGHTLIFE

EOL ROOFTOP BAR

Named after the powerful Greek god of the wind, this rooftop bar offers everything from breakfast coffees to cool DJ sets and a great party atmosphere. *Daily 8am–midnight | Fošal ulica 2 | FB: eolbar*

AROUND OMIŠ

18 CETINA GORGE

18km to Penšići / 30 mins by car

This forested valley is an attractive destination for hikers and cyclists. Rafting and canoe trips through the gorge from *Penšići* are also popular and two hours paddling will bring you to the restaurant *Radmanove mlinice (tel. 021 862 073 | radmanove-mlinice.hr | €€)*, a renovated mill serving excellent meat and fish (including local trout). Rafting excursions are available from e.g. *Kentona (approx. 35 euros| Drage Ivaniševića 15 | no phone | rafting-cetina.com).* 🚶 H5

MAKARSKA RIVIERA

🚶 *J 5–6* **The coastal road at the foot of the Biokovo mountains winds tightly around coves and fjords, running past tiny fishing villages, fragrant scrub, vineyards and the palm-lined promenades of bathing resorts.**

The mountain range is what gives the ★ *Makarska Riviera* its mild climate, acting as a shield against the icy gusts of the Bora, while the islands of Brač, Hvar and Korčula protect the coast from the waves of the sea. With such a high degree of natural protection, it was inevitable that the riviera

Towering over the Makarska Riviera is the Biokovo peak Sveti Jure

would become a holiday destination. Alongside modern hotel complexes there are plenty of campsites.

PLACES ON THE MAKARSKA RIVIERA

🔟 BIOKOVO MOUNTAINS

This steep, dry, barren landscape, part of the Dinaric Alps, is a protected natural park *(admission approx. 7 euros | biokovo.com)* although at first glance it seems almost devoid of vegetation. However, closer inspection reveals a surprising variety of flora, including countless endemic species which you can also see in the large *Botanical Garden* in *Kotišina (located above the village | free entry)*. Hiking trails pass through thick beech and pine forests, skirting crevasses and caves, old stone churches and the remnants of fortifications. A narrow, exposed road leads up to the summit of *Sv. Jure* (1,762m), the highest mountain in the Biokovo. The peak can be scaled in around two hours from the *Dom Vošac* hut – a 450-m ascent. 🗺 *J5–6*

🔟 MAKARSKA

Like most of the older settlements along the riviera, Makarska (pop. 13,500) comprises an upper section spread along the side of the mountain and a lower town. The two have now merged into a single resort, centred on the lively shoreline promenade. The historic centre spreads around *Trg F. A. Kačića*, where the belltower of the 18th-century *Sv. Marko* church rises decoratively in front of the rocky backdrop of the Biokovo mountains. A few

Baroque *Palazzi* are preserved, including those built by the Ivanišević family (*Trg F. A. Kačića*) and the Tonoli family (*Obala kralja Tomislava 16*). The Franciscan monastery is home to the *Malakološki muzej (Mon–Sat 10am–noon, 5–7pm, Sun 10am–noon | about 2 euros | Franjevački put 1)*, which contains a rich collection of snails and shellfish.

INSIDER TIP
Sea of canvas

Nearby, at Imagine Art (Kalalarga 1) you can admire sealife through the eyes of artist Marijeta Lozina.

Makarska's 🏖 2-km beach runs around the bay to the north of the centre. There is also the beautiful *Osejava* park south of the old town – its shade makes it great for strolls and runs. Just beyond it is *Nugal* nudist beach. A comprehensive range of sporting activities such as parasailing, windsurfing and diving is available; see for instance *Parasailing Makarska (Put Cvitačke 2a | tel. 098 963 1918)* or the diving centre *More Sub (K.P. Krešimira 43 | tel. 021 611 727 | more-sub-makarska.hr)*.

Lots of restaurants and taverns compete for customers, offering Dalmatian cuisine and terraces with sea views. *Ivo (Ante Starčevića 41 | tel. 021 611 257 | €–€€)* is located in town away from the waterfront; but what it lacks in views it more than makes up for with its food. If you don't want to forego the sight of the waves, then try *DiVino (Šetalište F. Tuđmana | tel. 099 410 2153 | €€€)*, an ultra-stylish restaurant with prices that are very reasonable considering its quality and location. The *Wine Bar Grabovac (Trg*

The authentic side of Makarska, away from the crowds of tourists and beach entertainment

F.A. Kačića | tel. 098 934 1226) is a popular place to stop for an early-evening aperitif or a small snack before moving on elsewhere. *Deep Makarska (daily 9am–5am | Šetalište fra Jure Radića 5a | deep.hr)* is a great bar and club housed in a seaside cave. 🕮 J6

NORTH OF MAKARSKA

Just under 10km to the north, the village of *Bratuš*, with its old stone houses and its small cove, is like travelling back in time. The *Konoba Bratuš (Bratuš 46 | tel. 021 548 548 | €)* directly on the waterfront offers friendly service and good cuisine.

The skyline around *Baška Voda* is dominated by the imposing Biokovo mountains; a wide selection of bars and restaurants can be found close together on the shingle beach. In *Palac (Obala Sv. Nikole 2 | tel. 021 620 544 | €€)* you can sit under shady trees and tuck into fresh seafood. Experienced divers can make a trip out to the *Vruja gorges* where freshwater meets colourful coral. Agents include the *Poseidon Diving Center (Blato 13, diving-poseidon.hr)*.

Nearby *Brela* has shingle beaches, gastronomic offerings and sporting activities for unbridled holiday fun. The rocky island of *Kamen Brela*, off the main beach of ⚲ *Dugi rat*, has a thick covering of pine trees and is popular among photographers. Formerly known by the name *Punta rata*, this beach is often very busy in the summer. ⚲ The shingle slopes so gently into the sea that it has become very popular with families as children can swim very safely. There are trees for shade and lots of cafés with tasty child-friendly snacks. Fresh fish at fair prices is available at *Konoba Feral (Obala Kneza Domagoja 30 | tel. 021 618 909 | €€)*. 📖 *J5–6*

SOUTH OF MAKARSKA

Tučepi is directly connected to Makarska and differs little from the riviera's main town. Here you will find *Nugal Beach*, a famous nudist beach shielded from prying eyes by steep rocky cliffs. Head uphill for 45 minutes to reach *Gornji Tučepi*, home to a gourmet's paradise with glorious views: *Restaurant Jeny (Gornji Tučepi 33 | tel. 091 587 8078 | restaurant-jeny.hr | €€€)* serves fine modern interpretations of Dalmatian cuisine.

Živogošće is shielded from winds blowing from the country's interior by the 1,155-m *Sutvid*; here, the mountains come so close to the shore that idyllic beaches, such as *Mala Duba*, practically nestle under the rock face. Accommodation is available in private rooms. 📖 *J6*

AROUND THE MAKARSKA RIVIERA

🔟 BLUE & RED LAKES

35km from Makarska / 45 mins inland by car

It's well worth leaving the beach for a day to take a very special dip in the *Modro jezero (Blue Lake)*, north of Imotski. Although you can't always swim in the karst lake (it can dry up in summer), it's impressive whatever time of year you come and you may even catch the locals playing a game of football on the lake bed. The lake lies in a 900-m-deep sinkhole and there's a paved footpath leading down to the bottom.

Its neighbour, the *Red Lake (Crveno jezero)*, is in fact not red at all – it takes its name from the red cliffs which surround it. *From the south side of the Blue Lake, drive northwest along the road for approx. 1km.* 📖 *J5*

The Red Lake takes its name from the surrounding cliffs

DUBROVNIK REGION

A LIVING RENAISSANCE WORK OF ART

Walk through ancient coastal towns accompanied by the scent of oranges, rosemary and the sea. This is southern Dalmatia at its most alluring.

The southernmost region in Croatia is made up of a narrow strip of land between the Dinaric mountains and the coast. It is cut off from the rest of Dalmatia in the north by Bosnia's narrow strip of coast and in the south it borders Montenegro.

Dubrovnik Old Town and the island of Lokrum

Dubrovnik's impressive walls and towers attract tourists from all over the world, but the islands around it are every bit as rich in atmosphere and history. Head to Mljet and follow in Odysseus's footsteps; retrace Marco Polo's route through Korčula; or taste Pelješac's excellent red wine. Then dive into the sea in a bay on the Elphatiti Islands, surrounded by abandoned villas and beautiful gardens. It's a place to discover and savour.

DUBROVNIK REGION

HRVATSKA

Makarska

Brač

Stari Grad

Hvar

Proizd

7 Vela Luka

6 Blato

Korčula ★ 4

Lumbarda 5 Pržina

Korčula
p. 99

1 Orebić

Pelješac
p. 96

Neretva Delta 11

Plo

8 Lastovo

40km, 30 mins

MARCO POLO HIGHLIGHTS

★ **MLJET**
This small, romantic island is reputed to have enchanted Odysseus ➤ p. 98

★ **KORČULA TOWN**
A picturesque town that boasts of being Marco Polo's birthplace ➤ p. 100

★ **DUBROVNIK'S FORTIFICATIONS**
Huge bastions, towers and cannons protect Dubronik's magnificent old town ➤ p. 104

★ **SPONZA PALACE**
This splendid city palace in Dubrovnik perfectly combines Gothic and Renaissance elements ➤ p. 107

★ **ARBORETUM TRSTENO**
Glorious subtropical plants, a Renaissance villa and a pier, not to mention a relaxing atmosphere and a crystal-clear sea to swim in ➤ p. 112

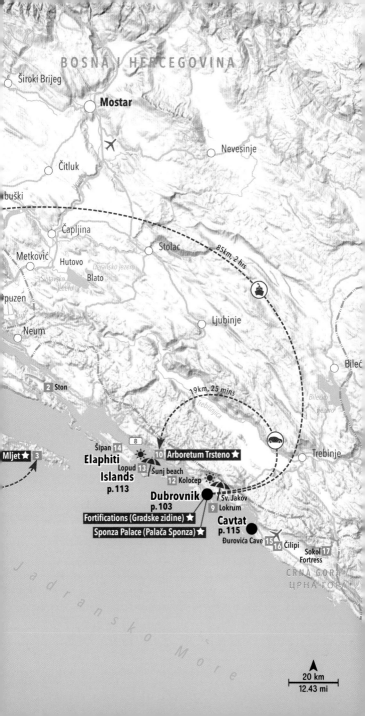

BOSNA I HERCEGOVINA

Široki Brijeg

Mostar

Čitluk

Nevesinje

buški

Čapljina

Stolac

85km, 2 hrs

Metković

Hutovo

Deransko jezero

Svitavsko jezero

Blato

Ljubinje

puzen

Neum

Bileć

Bilećko jezero

2 Ston

19km, 25 mins

Trebišnjica

Mljet **★** **3**

Šipan **14**

Elaphiti
Islands
p. 113

Lopud

13

Šunj beach

10 **Arboretum Trsteno ★**

8

12 Koločep

Trebinje

Dubrovnik
p. 103

7 Sv. Jakov

9 Lokrum

Fortifications (Gradske zidine) ★

Sponza Palace (Palača Sponza) ★

Cavtat
p. 115

Đurovića Cave

15

16 Čilipi

Sokol **17**
Fortress

CRNA GORA
ЦРНА ГОРА

Jadransko More

▲
20 km
12.43 mi

PELJEŠAC

J–K 6–7 **The peninsula of Pelješac is connected to the mainland by a narrow isthmus. The farmers here primarily produce wine and olives, as they do on the island of Korčula, which runs almost parallel to Pelješac.**

The acquisition of the island by Ragusa in 1333 was something of a coup for the city state as it provided a base directly opposite Korčula, which belonged to its rival Venice. Ragusa equipped this precious territory with a 7km defensive wall equipped with three forts, 41 towers, seven bastions, four ramparts and a moat – creating in the process Europe's largest fortification. The wall closed off overland access to both the peninsula and the profitable salt works near Veliki Ston.

The 65-km²-long peninsula (pop. 10,000) is very sparsely populated. Beaches and resorts can mainly be found along the flat northern coast, while the south coast is made up of rugged cliffs. A number of small roads carved boldly into the rock face or running through tunnels come off the main road and lead to tiny wine-growing villages. In spite of the stony, barren soils, this is where one of the most famous of Dalmatia's wines, *Dingač*, is produced. You might even spot jackals prowling across the vineyards in the early morning. Discovery Tour 3 will take you to meet some of the local vintners and olive growers (see p. 128).

PLACES ON PELJEŠAC

1 OREBIĆ

This town (pop. 2,000) at the foot of the 1,000-m mountain Sv. Ilija has a proud history as an important merchant navy base which boasted over 60 ships during the 19th century. The captains of the ships invested their profits in prestigious villas, in whose gardens they planted exotic souvenirs from their journeys across the world. Memories of this era are preserved at the *Maritime Museum (Pomorski muzej | Mon–Fri 7am–8pm, Sat/Sun 6–8pm, winter Mon–Fri 7am–3pm | about 2 euros | Trg Mimbelli).*

Modern Orebić is a sleepy but charming town. The pretty beaches to the west and northeast of the village are great for children, especially *Trstenica* beach, while active visitors will relish the thrill of racing down the *Pelješki* strait on a surfboard with the steady Maestral wind at their backs.

The monastery *Gospa od Anđela (summer Mon–Sat 9am–noon, 4–7pm | about 3 euros | Celestinov put 6),* built on a hill overlooking the town during the 15th century, provides a reminder of the Cold War between the rival maritime powers of Venice and Ragusa. From here, Ragusan lookouts would surveil the goings-on in Venetian Korčula. An atmospheric cloister, a Renaissance relief of the Madonna and Child by Nikola Firentinac, and the tranquil cemetery containing the graves of sea captains are all well worth a look.

The chef at the Restaurant *Babilon (Đivovićeva 2 | tel. 020 713 352 | €€)*

has a good understanding of classic Dalmatian cuisine. The view from the restaurant *Panorama (summer only, from 5pm | Celestinov put | no tel.| €€)*, on the road leading up to the monastery, is genuinely stunning. Grilled dishes make up most of the menu here.

The neighbouring village of *Viganj* is a mecca for wind- and kitesurfers. The water-sport centre *Water Donkey (tel. 091 152 0258 | windsurfing-kitesurfing-viganj.com)* rents out surfing equipment, as well as bikes *(13 euros/day)* and stand-up paddleboards or kayaks *(about 18 euros/day)*. The strait between Pelješac and Korčula is a great place for 👶 kids to learn too and you can book a four-day

course *(children's course approx. 80 euros | Ponta | Viganj | liberansurf.eu)*. This is perfect place to learn how to windsurf. After a full day of activities you can party the night away at bar *Karmela 2*. ⌖ *J7*

2 STON

Ston – which consists of the two villages of *Veliki* (Greater) and *Mali* (Lesser) Ston – is where the Pelješac peninsula joins the mainland on an isthmus measuring only 1,500m across. Both villages are encircled by a 14th-century *defensive wall (April/May, Aug/Sept daily 8am–6.30pm; June/July 8am–7.30pm, Oct 8am–5.30pm;*

Explore the coast near Orebić

Nov–March 8am–3pm | about 7 euros | citywallsdubrovnik.hr/bastina/stonske-zidine) that climbs steeply over the hills that lie between them. This monumental structure was severely damaged by an earthquake in 1996 but, thanks to renovation works, visitors can now walk along 5.5km of the walls. Having said that, it is best to avoid this walk under the heat of the midday sun, as there is absolutely no shade to be found along the route.

The *salt works (summer daily 10am–7pm; winter 7am–2pm | about 2 euros | Pelješki put 1 | solanaston.hr)* here still produce salt using traditional methods, while the mussels and oysters cultivated in the shallow waters before Mali Ston are served freshly prepared at *Bota Šare (Mali Ston | tel. 020 754 482 | bota-sare.hr | €€€). Papratno*, to the south, is a gorgeous beach with a large campsite. *K7*

AROUND PELJEŠAC

3 MLJET ⭐
45 mins on the Prapratno–Sobra car ferry

Mljet's history starts with Odysseus, who was allegedly detained here by Calypso. There followed successive waves of Romans and Illyrians and, although the island lies a long way from Puglia's coast, monks from Puglia settled here in the 12th century. The western half of the island (pop. 1,100) is a protected *national park (admission about 9.50 euros, in peak season about 17 euros | Pristanište 2 | Goveđari-Mljet | tel. 020 744 041 | np-mljet.hr).* Mljet has a varied landscape and its rugged south coast contrasts with a series of coves along the north coast. There is a lot to see underwater as well – in 2017, 150 amphorae dating back to the first century were discovered here. Divers are invited to dive under netting (in place to protect the treasures from being stolen) to admire the finds. The ports of *Sobra, Polače* and *Pomena* and the other villages on the island give the impression that time has stood still here. Mljet is still a destination for more adventurous travellers, and accommodation is found primarily in private rooms.

The main attraction in the national parks in the thickly forested west are the salt lakes *Veliko* and *Malo jezero*. Southeast of the latter on an island accessible by ferry is the Benedictine monastery of *Sv. Marija*. Ferries leave from *Pristanište* or from the *Mali most* bridge every hour from 9am until 7pm during the summer. The small complex was built in the 12th century but was altered in the Renaissance, and the restaurant *Melita (Otok Sv. Marije | Veliko jezero | tel. 020 744 145 | €€)* has a great location within the monastery walls. A short walk will take you past the picturesque cemetery.

Bikes and boats for a tour around or on the lakes can be rented from *Radulj Tours (tel. 098 428 074)* by the *Mali most* bridge, and scooters are available for about 35 euros per day at

According to local legend, Calypso held Odysseus captive in this cave

Mini Brun (Sobra 33 | tel. 020 745 084 | rent-a-car-scooter-mljet.hr) in *Sobra*. From *Polače*, you can hike up the highest hill on the island, *Montokuc* (253m). Here you can enjoy stunning views over Korčula, Lastovo and Pelješac before returning to Polače past Veliko jezero and Pristanište (around three hours, clearly signposted).

Just south of the national park there is a well-hidden piece of ancient history: the 🐖 mythical Odysseus Cave which you can either reach by boat or on a half-hour walk (in sensible shoes) from Babino Polje, before diving into the water and swimming into the cave itself. The light in the mornings there is fantastic. *K7*

INSIDER TIP
Follow in the steps of Odysseus

KORČULA

H–J7 **The island of Korčula (pop. 17,000) is just under 50km long, and, as one of Dalmatia's most important regions for olive oil and wine production, it has a strong emphasis on agriculture – particularly in its eastern half. The west has lots of small coves, surrounded by trees. The island's capital, also called Korčula, is a charming miniature version of Dubrovnik.**

The lengthy periods of foreign domination that punctuate the history of Dalmatia are plain to see in the towns on the island – especially Korčula town. The island was governed by Venice from 1427 until it was conquered by Napoleon in 1797. This led to a certain degree of tension, however, as the neighbouring peninsula of *Pelješac* belonged to Venice's main enemy Ragusa. The border between the two ran through the 1.3km-wide strait *Pelješki* – a strait now popular with windsurfers. The island's superb olives oils and wines – including the fruity white varieties *Pošip* and *Grk* and the fiery red *Plavac Mali* – can be sampled on Discovery Tour 3 (see p. 128).

PLACES ON KORČULA

4 KORČULA ★ ⚑

Viewed from above, Korčula town (pop. 5,600) looks like the foredeck of a ship protruding into the sea on its peninsula and intersected from north to south by the main street *Korčulanskog statua*. A series of lanes branch off from it on the left and right, all leading to the sea. Fresh easterly and westerly winds blow through the town, acting like natural air con. Although Korčula received its very modern layout during the 13th century, it had already had a long and turbulent history involving previous Greek, Roman and Slavic settlements. The late Medieval and Renaissance buildings of the town are remarkably well preserved.

The main street leads gently uphill past the *Town Hall* and the *Sv. Mihovil chapel* (both dating from 1525) to its highest point, *Trg Sv. Marko* (St Mark's Square). This square is dominated by the 15th-century *Katedrala Sv. Marka*, whose portal features two Gothic lions. Inside, an early Tintoretto painting, late-Gothic masonry and a modern bronze of Sv. Vlaho by Ivan Meštrović all somehow create a sense of harmony. Next to the cathedral, the 19th-century *Bishop's Palace (May–Sept Mon–Sat 9am–7pm; Oct 9am–2pm | about 3.50 euros)* contains a rich selection of ecclesiastical treasures and paintings. The *Renaissance Palace Gabrieli* opposite is home to the *City Museum (Oct–March daily 10am–2pm, April–June daily 10am–1pm; July-Sept daily 9am–9pm | about 3 euros)* which displays archaeological artefacts, naval instruments, the household objects of a Renaissance family and much more besides.

A bit further along Ismaeli ulica, you will find an old city gate which contains the fun and modern *Vapor Gallery (Mon–Sat 10am–10.30pm, Sun 1–10.30pm | Kula Morska Vrata)*. There are plenty of grand palaces to be seen as you stroll through the streets of the town, and inevitably you will come across the late-Gothic ruin of *Marco Polo's House (Kuća Marka Pola)*. The famous explorer is said to have been born here in 1254, but there is little proof beyond the fact that "Dapolo" is a common surname on the island. There are a few historical documents on show here. The *Marko Polo muzej (daily April/May 10am–3pm; June–Sept 9am–11pm; Oct/Nov 10am–3pm | about 8 euros | Plokata 14. travnja 1921)* is much more interesting, with models and an accompanying audio guide explaining the different stages of Marco Polo's life.

Sv. Marka Cathedral contains artistic treasures from centuries gone by

At *Aterina (Trg Korčulanskih klesara i kipara 1 | tel. 091 986 1856 | €€€)* the personable chef demonstrates his talent with modern interpretations of Dalmatian cuisine.

INSIDER TIP
Sweet souvenirs

Komparak (Plokota 19 | tel. 091 434 3413) sells genuine regional produce such as fig jam and honey and the owner is only too happy to tell you all about his bees.

You can also visit the beehives, olive groves and animals, as well as taste some of the food. Guided tours are available in English. In the evenings, the perfect place to watch the sunset is the restaurant at *Maksimilijan Garden (Sveti Nikola | tel. 091 170 2567 | €–€€)*.

5 LUMBARDA

Greek colonists from the island of *Vis* founded Lumbarda (pop. 1,200) as early as the fourth century BCE. During the 14th and 15th centuries, nobles from Korčula built country houses here, a few of which have been restored and can still be seen among the green vineyards that produce a fine white wine called *Grk*. The small harbour and historical centre are surrounded by attractive coves – including the large, popular sandy beach in the cove of *Pržina*. Accommodation is primarily in private rooms and apartments. The sustainably minded might like to stay at *Agroturizam Bire (tel. 020 712 007 | bire.hr)*, where they also produce delicious wine *(Grk and Plavac Mali)* grown in line with the

Lumbarda's vineyards produce excellent white wine

very strictest organic principles. The *Konoba More (Bilin Zal | tel. 020 712 068 | €€)* serves grilled meat and fish on a pretty terrace overlooking the sea.

Take a detour to *Žrnovo* (8km) where you can try the regional pasta speciality *Žrnovski makaruni* – best of all at *Konoba Belin (Žrnovo 50 | reservation recommended: tel. 091 503 9258 | €€)*. You can try your hand at pasta rolling in the cookery course held at the *konoba* (about 25 euros per person including food). The 400-year-old recipe is celebrated every August at the Makarunada festival.

INSIDER TIP
Make-your-own cheese

6 BLATO

Blato (pop. 4,000) is known for its 1-km-long boulevard of lime trees. The main square's grandest buildings are a free-standing *loggia* and a *parish church* (14th century) with a side chapel dedicated to the town's patron St Vincenca. On her saint's day, 28 April, a local folklore group performs the traditional *kumpanija* sword dance outside the church.

The delicious meals served in the cosy inner courtyard of the *Konoba Zlinje (Ulica 85 6/1 | tel. 020 851 050 | €)* are made using regional products – the fish is especially good. *H7*

7 VELA LUKA

Korčula's second-largest settlement (pop. 4,500) looks out to the west and the open sea. Of the multiple shipyards once found here, only one has survived: the *Montmontaža Greben*, where lifeboats are built. The *Cultural Centre (summer Mon–Fri 8am–3pm, Sat 9am–1pm | 2 euros)* houses archaeological discoveries that were made in the nearby *Vela spilja* cave *(velaspila.hr)*, with artefacts dating back to the Neolithic period over 20,000 years ago. With permission from the museum, it is possible to visit the cave, located around 2km away.

The beaches close to the town are not particularly noteworthy, but a trip to the neighbouring island of *Proizd* is a must: its turquoise waters are among the most beautiful in Croatia. Get there via water taxi or by hiring a kayak or motorboat *(Vela Luka Rent | kayak about 30 euros/day, boat from about 47 euros/day | tel. 098 954 0388 | velalukarent.com)*. You can then round off your day by dining on fresh fish and shellfish in the *Konoba Lučica (Ulica 51 | tel. 020 813 673 | €€)*.

undiscovered divers' dream with its steep cliffs and diverse marine life. Trips can be organised through

INSIDER TIP
Unknown underwater world

Diving Center Ankora (Zaklopatica 46 | tel. 020 801 170 | lastovo-diving-ankora.com).

Visit the main village of *Lastovo* to see the island's typical chimneys, whose size and rich detailing testify to the former prosperity of the houses' owners. The best beach is *Skrivena luka*, the "hidden harbour" on the south coast. *Konoba Augusta Insula (Zaklopatica | tel. 098 571 884 | augustainsula.com | €€€)* serves excellent fish and homegrown vegetables in a grandish setting right on the water. Those arriving by boat can moor right outside. ⌖ *H–J7*

AROUND KORČULA

🔳 LASTOVO
1.5 hrs Vela Luka–Ubli car ferry

Visitors to this island to the south of Korčula will feel as if they've reached paradise. Beautiful bays, crystal-clear water, verdant Mediterranean greenery, olive groves and three small villages with around 800 inhabitants make this a calm, relaxing place to get away from it all. Because it lies at the centre of a protected archipelago of 44 islands, Lastovo is a good base for the *Lastovo National Park (pp-lastovo. hr)*. This nature reserve is an

DUBROVNIK

⌖ *L7* **Visitors have to make their way past crooked city gates and mighty bastions before they can fall under the spell of this bright and elegant city (pop. 42,000).**

Having said that, it's the fully preserved city wall that contributes a large part of Dubrovnik's charm, and visitors will feel themselves transported back through the centuries to a time when Ragusa defied both the city republic of Venice and the Ottoman Empire without ever being conquered. Perhaps it's more accurate to say that Ragusa played its opponents off against each other. Ragusa's strength

was its tightly interlinked and far-reaching network of diplomatic and trade relations, and its military endeavours were limited to making the city unconquerable. Even Napoleon, who plundered Ragusa's treasures in 1806, was unable to breach Dubrovnik's fortifications; the city gates were opened to him instead. Today, Dubrovnik is entirely devoted to tourism which, of course, brings both pros and cons. On the one hand, the majority of locals make their livelihood from tourists but on the other, the hordes of people can overwhelm the city in summer.

To retain its status as a World Heritage Site, UNESCO has appealed to the city to reduce the number of tourists. The "Pearl of the Adriatic" is becoming harder and ever more expensive to admire so it is best to visit out of peak season. Dubrovnik has now reduced the number of cruise ships that can stop here (max. 4,000 guests per day) but nonetheless it is worth checking their arrival times at *portdubrovnik.hr.*

INSIDER TIP
Keep clesr of the cruise ships

☛ The Dubrovnik Card *(about 26 euros/day | dubrovnikcard.com)* gives you free or reduced admission to most museums as well as free public transport.

SIGHTSEEING

FORTIFICATIONS (GRADSKE ZIDINE) ★

The 1,940-m-long *City Wall* was vastly expanded by the city elders during

Ulica Bruna Bušića

simira IV

eša

Lazareti

Museum
of Contemporary Art
(Umjetnička
galerija Dubrovnik)

100 m
109 yd

the 15th and 16th centuries. The best architects of the age – Juraj Dalmatinac from Zadar, Michelozzo Michelozzi from Florence and the Ragusan Paskoje Miličević – reinforced the monumental structure with five forts, 16 towers, 120 cannons and two main gates: the *Pile Gate* in the west and the *Ploče Gate* in the east. The two-hour walk around the tops of the walls forcefully conveys just how impregnable the defences must have seemed to attackers, and there are plenty of good views (and photo opportunities) over the old town. The main entrance can be found next to the Pile Gate; two other access points are by *Sv. Luka* church and *Sv. Ivan Fortress*. The route runs anti-clockwise only.

☂ *Sv. Ivan Fortress* was built in the 14th and 15th centuries to protect Ragusa's port, now known as the Old Harbour. You can see the fortifications from the inside here, as the basement contains an attractive *Aquarium (May/June and Sept/Oct daily 9am-7pm; July/Aug daily 9am-9pm; Nov-April Mon-Sat 9am-1pm | about 8 euros)*, displaying Mediterranean flora and fauna in 20 tanks. The rooms above contain a *Maritime Museum (Nov-March Tue-Sun 9am-4pm; April-Oct Tue-Sun 9am-6pm | 6 euros)* explaining Ragusa's naval history. The bulky Renaissance *Fort Lovrijenac* stands on a 37m spur of rock in front of the western wall. It might well look familiar. In the TV show *Game of Thrones* it doubles as King's Landing, the capital of the Seven Kingdoms. *April/May and Aug/Sept daily 8am-6.30pm; June/July daily 8am-7.30pm; Oct daily 8am-5.30pm; Nov-March daily 9am-3pm | joint ticket fortifications, Sv. Ivan Fortress and Fort Lovrijenac about 20 euros, museums cost extra, joint museum ticket 16 euros | ⊙ 1.5 hrs*

Not far from Lovrijenac lies the *Love*

WHERE TO START?

From **Pile Gate**, in the west of the old town near the tourist information centre, you come straight into the historic centre and the route along the city walls. Parking is possible in **Iza Grada**, along the northern city walls, or at **Gradac Park**, west of the old town. There are buses to Pile Gate from the bus station on Gruž harbour *(Obala Ivana Pavla II)*.

Enjoy shopping and sightseeing as you stroll along Stradun

Stories Museum (daily 10am–6pm | Od Tabakarije 2 | about 7 euros | lovestories museum.com). Yes, it's kitsch and corny, but it is also very sweet indeed.

GREAT ONOFRIO FOUNTAIN (VELIKA ONOFRIJEVA FONTANA)

This polygonal fountain built near the Pile Gate in 1438 has sustained a great deal of damage over the years and, aside from its 16 cisterns (or *maškeron*), is almost devoid of ornament. It formed the end point of an 11km-long water pipe leading from a spring into the city – a technological masterpiece created by the architect Onofrio della Cava. Another smaller fountain once supplied the Luža market square.

FRANCISCAN PRIORY (FRANJEVAČKI SAMOSTAN)

The monastery by the Pile Gate was founded in the 14th century and left in ruins by the devastating earthquake of 1667. However, its fantastic cloister escaped damage almost completely, meaning that visitors can still marvel at the grotesque figures and mythical creatures that adorn its column capitals. The monks here operated a pharmacy in 1317, making it one of the oldest in Europe. It is still preserved inside the monastery in its early 20th-century form. *Summer daily 9am–6pm; Nov–March 9am–5pm | about 4 euros | Placa 2 | godubrovnik.guide/ short.travel/ kkd6 | ⊙ 1 hr*

STRADUN (PLACA)

This 300-m-long street – known to residents as *Placa* – runs from the Pile Gate to the former market square Luža. Its path follows that of the channel that used to separate the originally Slavic settlement of Dubrovnik on the mainland from the post-Roman island of Ragusa, before it was filled in during the 11th century. A devastating earthquake destroyed the city in 1667, and the reconstruction gave the Placa its uniform look, as the City Council imposed strict rules governing the height and appearance of the new buildings. Nowadays the marble-paved street is lined with cafés and boutiques, and in the evenings people come here to promenade along the lively *korzo*.

SYNAGOGUE

Dubrovnik's Jewish community lived in the ghetto around *Žudioska ulica* (Jewry Street) from the 15th century onwards. This simple synagogue is the only surviving building from the old ghetto. Historical documents and photographs recall the city's Jewish community, the majority of whom were deported from Dubrovnik during the Fascist occupation in the Second World War. Today the Jewish community numbers not many more than 30 members. *May–Oct daily 10am–8pm; winter Mon–Fri 10am–3pm | about 6 euros | Žudioska ulica 5 | ⊙ 30 mins.*

SPONZA PALACE
(PALAČA SPONZA) ★

The Placa was originally lined with buildings in the same style as this palazzo, with Venetian Gothic ground-floor arcades and first-floor windows, and Renaissance elements on the upper floors. Decorative, elegant and simply perfect. The 1667 earthquake damaged the Sponza Palace, which was used as a customs house at the time. However, it was repaired, allowing this wonderful example of Ragusan architecture to survive to the present day. Nowadays it contains the city archive, as well as a memorial to the victims of the Siege of Dubrovnik by Yugoslavian troops in 1991–92. One hundred and fourteen civilians died during this nine-month siege. A large part of the historic building was destroyed and had to be reconstructed – the new bright-red roof slates symbolize this effort. Just a few streets further is the *War Photo Limited Gallery (daily 10am–10pm | about 7 euros | Antuninska 6)*, which exhibits moving war photos. Opposite the Sponza Palace stands the Orlando Column, erected in 1418; the statue's forearm was used to set the standard length of the Ragusan cubit (51.2cm). At the western end of the palace is the 31m Clock Tower (1444), whose two bronze figures strike the bell every hour. The original figures are on display in the Rector's Palace. ⊙ *45 mins*

DOMINICAN MONASTERY
(DOMINIKANSKI SAMOSTAN)

This is an idyllic spot with palm trees and an orangery. This monastery situated on the approach to the Ploče Gate was founded in 1225, and in the 16th century an enchanting cloister was added to it. The monastery's gallery is also worth a visit – particularly its 16th-century Nikola Božidarević triptych, which shows St Blaise holding a model of Ragusa in his hands. *May–Oct daily 9am–6pm; winter 9am–5pm | about 4 euros | Svetog Dominika 4 | ⏱ 1 hr*

RECTOR'S PALACE (KNEŽEV DVOR)

Although the city governor's palace dates back to the 15th century with its typically Ragusan blend of Gothic and Renaissance styles, its current form is actually from the 17th and 18th centuries. The ground floor contains guard rooms and a dungeon, while the rector's apartments can be seen upstairs. Each rector was only elected for a one-month term, and during that period was not permitted to leave his quarters (this was to prevent anybody from influencing his judgment). *April–Oct daily 9am–6pm; Nov–March 9am–4pm | about 11 euros | Pred dvorom 1 | ⏱ 45 mins*

GUNDULIĆEVA POLJANA

This is one of the liveliest and most attractive squares in the old town; a market is held here every morning at the foot of the monument to the Ragusan poet Ivan Gundulić (1589–1638), next to the cathedral. Farmers from Konavle sell fruit, vegetables, honey and Dubrovnik's speciality: candied bitter orange peel (*arancini*).

RUPE ETHNOGRAPHIC MUSEUM (ETNOGRAFSKI MUZEJ RUPE)

The museum's collection of clothing and tools from Dubrovnik and the neighbouring Konavle valley is just as interesting as the building in which it is housed: an enormous 15th-century granary built directly into the city wall, in which Ragusa used to store its supplies. *April–Oct daily 9am–6pm; winter Mon–Sat 9am–2pm | 7-day museum pass (valid for 7 days and 8 museums) about 16 euros | Od Rupa 3 | dumus.hr | ⏱ 1 hr*

MUSEUM OF CONTEMPORARY ART (UMJETNIČKA GALERIJA DUBROVNIK)

Housed in the former residence of a rich ship-building family, this gallery is located just a few minutes away from the old town. It showcases over 300 works of contemporary art, including some by Dalmatian Art Nouveau painter Vlaho Bukovac. Splendid views of the old town can be enjoyed from the sculpture terrace. *Daily 9am–8pm 7-day museum pass (valid for 7 days and 8 museums) about 16 euros | Frana Supila 23 | ugdubrovnik. hr | ⏱ 1.5 hrs*

SRD

Once you get up there, the view from the restaurant *Nautika (Nov–March daily. 9am–4pm; April/May/Oct 9am–8pm, Sept 9am–10pm, June–Aug 9am–midnight | nautika restaurants.com/panorama-restaurant-bar)* on top of this 412m hill is simply stunning. The hill itself is both Dubrovnik's most beautiful viewpoint and a memorial to the Yugoslavian War in 1991–2. A 60-man unit stationed in *Fort Imperial* on its summit put up a spirited resistance to the much more numerous attacking forces during the Siege of Dubrovnik, and a museum *(winter daily 8am–4pm; summer 8am–6pm | about 4 euros)* inside the fort tells the story. Both the summit and the museum can be reached by car, on foot, or by means of a modern cable car *(Nov–March daily 9am–4pm, April/May/Oct 9am–8pm; Sept 9am–10pm; June–Aug 9am–midnight | return trip about 20 euros | Petra Krešimira 4 | dubrovnikcablecar.com).* | ⌑ L7

EATING & DRINKING

360

This exquisite restaurant with a great view of the old town combines traditional Mediterranean cuisine with French techniques. Reserve early. *Closed Mon and at lunch | Sv.Dominka bb | tel. 020 322 222 | 360dubrovnik. com | €€€*

It takes 3 minutes by cable car to the summit of Srđ

BARBA

Seafood and fish at affordable prices. At *Barba* in Dubrovnik you can buy seafood and fish at affordable prices to take away - e.g. in an octopus burger *(around 6 euros). Boškovićeva 5 | tel. 091 205 3488 | €*

FAST FOOD PREŠA 🍴

An oasis of good value in the pricey old town. Delicious sandwiches, *čevapčiči* and savoury pancakes. *Đordićeva 2 | €*

KAMENICA

A Dubrovnik institution: visit during the morning to feast on oysters and champagne (the main reason to come here) while enjoying a view over the lively market. *Gundulićeva poljana 8 | tel. 020 323 682 | €€*

KOPUN

On the square with the Jesuit church, this place serves excellent food – including dishes from other regions such as the capon from which it takes its name. Fans should definitely try the *Game of Thrones* set menu. *Poljana R. Boškovića 7 | tel. 020 323 969 | restaurantkopun.com | €€€*

INSIDER TIP
Eat like a *(Game of Thrones)* king

Sightseeing by kayak gives you a different perspective on Dubrovnik's old town

NISHTA

High-quality vegan food is almost impossible to find along the coast, which makes the creative dishes at this restaurant all the more special. Just a few minutes away from the Stradun, this place will convince even ardent carnivores. The brownies are great too. *Prijeko | tel. 020 322 088 | nishtarestaurant.com | €€*

STARA LOŽA

The restaurant in the *Prijeko Palace* hotel pulls in the punters with fine Mediterranean dining on the top floor of a Renaissance palace. You can also find an unusual tapas bar here. *Prijeko 22 | tel. 020 321 145 | €€€*

SHOPPING

The main shopping streets are the *Stadrun (Placa)* and the *Pred Dvorom* that branches off to the south; here you can find plenty of souvenir and fashion shops.

ART BY STJEPKO

The award-winning artist, Stjepko Mamić, has his studio just behind the Franciscan monastery. His mystic, ethereal paintings encapsulate Dubrovnik and its relationship to the sea. *Celestina Medovića 2 | stjepkomamic.com*

CHRISTMAS SHOP NOSTALGIJA

Fridge magnets out, handmade Christmas decorations in. How about a bauble with a Croatian flag on it? *Daily 8.30am–10pm | Nalješkovićeva 6 and Od Puča 9*

DEŠA

Embroidery, jams and honey produced by women from Konavle who were exiled and traumatised by the war. *Frana Supila 8 | in the Lazareti | desa-dubrovnik.hr*

DUBROVAČKA KUĆA

High-quality souvenirs such as excellent oil, Croatian wines and wonderful handicrafts. *Od Sv. Dominika*

KOKULA

Attractive handicrafts from the region, many of which are made in-house by this family company. *Đorđićeva 6*

SPORT & ACTIVITIES

ESCAPE ROOM 👕

Save the city in *Game of Thrones* or wander around the ruins of Dubrovnik after the 17th-century earthquake on the hunt for lost treasure. A lot of fun (and not just when it's raining). *2–5 players 25–33 euros/person | Josipa Kosora 22 | tel. 097 644 2145 | dubrovnikescaperoom.com*

KAYAKING

Paddling around the old town in a kayak makes for a wonderfully peaceful way to enjoy the views. Tours start from the bay beneath *Fort Lovrijenac. Adventure Dubrovnik (approx. 35 euros | Sv. Križa 3 | tel. 098 53 15 16 | adventuredubrovnik.com | ⏱ approx. 3 hrs)*

BEACHES

Close to the old town lies *Lokrum* island with its beautiful beaches (shingle and rock), as well as the sandy *Banje beach* near the Lazareti (Ploče Gate). Here you will also find the *East-West-Beach-Club (ew-dubrovnik.com)* with its luxurious loungers (approx. 14 euros) and DJ sets. There are more beaches near the touristy areas of *Lapad* and *Babin Kuk* (some charge admission).

NIGHTLIFE

BUŽA I & BUŽA II

These two bars on the rocks in front of the southern city wall are the places to go in Dubrovnik. You won't find a more relaxed place to enjoy a drink with a view of the sea. To get here, just follow the "cold drinks" signs. *Daily 8am–2am*

CULTURE CLUB REVELIN

Enjoy live gigs by Croatian pop stars and DJ parties over two floors in this historic fortress. *Daily 11pm–6am | Sv. Dominika | at the Ploče Gate | clubrevelin.com*

LAZARETI

This former plague quarantine camp has been transformed into a cultural centre containing art galleries and a nightclub. Parties and live concerts are organised to suit every music taste in

AROUND DUBROVNIK

this historic setting. They also a run a small arts *festival (lepetitfestival.com)* in June. You won't find a broader mix of arts in one place anywhere in the world – and especially not for free. Everything is included, from interpretative dance to Japanese tea ceremonies. *Frana Supila 8 | lazareti.com*

INSIDER TIP
Small but perfect

TROUBADOUR HARD JAZZ CAFÉ

The classic among the many café-bars on this square in the old town. Once just for jazz fans, nowadays it has opened itself up to include a broader set of musical tastes. *Daily 10am–2am | Bunićeva poljana 2*

Buža Bar

9 LOKRUM

15 mins from Dubrovnik by ferry

This tiny island lies just outside the Old Harbour. It owes its lushness to the Habsburg Archduke Maximilian, who planted the island with exotic trees and shrubs in the middle of the 19th century, and even introduced peacocks. Today, Lokrum is a protected nature reserve, and is a popular bathing spot among Dubrovnik's residents – its shady bays quickly fill up on summer weekends. Series fans are drawn by the small *Game of Thrones Museum (daily 11am–7pm | admission free)* inside the Benedictine abbey. Grab your chance to sit resplendent on the Iron Throne (it's the original from the set). A ferry service operates every 30 to 60 minutes from the Old Harbour. *📖 L8*

10 ARBORETUM TRSTENO ★

18km / 25 mins from Dubrovnik

A magical park created in the 15th century at the behest of a Ragusan noble family at their similarly well-preserved *Summer Palace*. Palm, eucalyptus, laurel, bougainvillea, oak and Aleppo pine surround statues, fountains and a villa. Once large ships from Ragusa stopped here; today it is visited by pleasure boats from Dubrovnik. If you brought your bathing costume then take a dip in these

INSIDER TIP
A posh place for a dip

opulent surroundings! A number of scenes for *Game of Thrones* were filmed here – it served as the royal family's garden. *May–Oct daily 7am–7pm; Nov–April 8am–4pm | about 7 euros | Potok 20 | short.travel/ kkd7 | ⏱ 30 mins | 🗺 L7*

🔟 NERETVA DELTA

65km / 1 hr 10 mins from Dubrovnik to Neum

The coastal mountain range opens up between *Neum* and *Ploče* to make room for the 280km Neretva river. At the mouth to the Adriatic Sea, it creates a wide delta. In "Croatian California" mandarins grow on trees

SIDER TIP
Vitamin C straight from the tree

as if it were the Garden of Eden. You can even roll up your sleeves and join in the mandarin harvest; people come from Dubrovnik and Makarska to lend a hand with the picking. The frogs and eels from this former swamp region were once seen as poor-man's food; today they are sold as a delicacy. Try a Neretva stew (*brudet*) in the restaurant *Đuda i Mate* (Vid | tel. 020 687 500 | djudjaimate. hr | €€). 🗺 K6

ELAPHITI ISLANDS

🗺 *L7* **A string of 13 islands – three of which are inhabited – lie one after another along the coast of South Dalmatia. The Greek sailors** who traded along the coast called them the Deer Islands (*elaphos* meaning "deer"). *Koločep*, *Lopud* and *Šipan* are particularly popular with adventurous visitors, thanks to their rich vegetation, tiny island villages and secluded coves.**

Wealthy ship owners and nobles from Ragusa erected palaces and fortresses on the islands during the city state's golden age. Most of these have now fallen into disrepair, but the examples that have been preserved are hugely impressive. The Elaphiti Islands are mostly car-free, making them the perfect destination for visitors who want to get away from it all and explore isolated routes and trails.

PLACES IN THE ELAPHITI ISLANDS

🔢 KOLOČEP

The island of Koločep (pop. 165) measures 2.4km², and of the three inhabited Elaphiti Islands it is the one most oriented towards tourism. Nonetheless, the largely English holidaymakers that come here mainly find accommodation in privately rented apartments. An attractive 3-km walking trail runs through olive groves and pine forests between the villages of Gornje Čelo and Donje Čelo. The vegetation here is mostly wild, although traces of former Ragusan gardens and ruined villas can still be found here and there. The path along the rugged northwest coast – also wonderful – offers enthralling and constantly changing views. Guests on the terrace of the beautiful restaurant

Villa Ruža (May–Sept only | Donje Čelo | tel. 020 757 030 | villa-ruza.com | €€) will be treated to amazing sunset views. *L7*

🔟 LOPUD

The village of *Lopud* (pop. 400), the arrival point for ferries, welcomes visitors with a picturesque view of its oval harbour lined with a monastery, palaces and old captain's houses. Renovation works at the Franciscan monastery have been underway for years now, and the former *Rector's Palace* and the palace of the Đorđić-Mayneri family with its palm garden are in a sad state of repair. Modern contrast is provided by *Your Black Horizon*, an installation by Icelandic artist Oliafur Eliasson *(mid-May–Sept daily 10am–7pm | admission free)*, which stands among the ruins.

An attractive walking trail runs past the Hotel Lafodia to the *Benešin rat* cape, where a *pavilion* offers views of the neighbouring island Šipan. A major attraction of Lopud is 🏖 *Šunj*, the child-friendly sandy beach of on the northern coast. It's a 20-minute walk across the island to the beach, and facilities include parasol rental and a small snack bar. *L7*

🔢 ŠIPAN

Measuring 14.5km² and with 500 inhabitants, Šipan is the largest and most populous of the Elaphiti Islands and it is perhaps the most interesting too. The island used to be a base for Ragusan nobles and wealthy ship owners, but almost all of its 60 villas and palaces have fallen into disrepair, as have the many old Croatian chapels that testify to an early Slavic settlement. Their ruins are scarcely visible under the rampant vegetation. The two villages of *Šipanska Luka* in the east and *Suđurad* in the west are linked by a fertile and intensively farmed karst valley, along which the island's bus service runs (in coordination with the ferry). Unlike Lopud, Šipan lacks any wide beachy coves; instead, visitors will need to wander along the coast to one of the small rocky coves, or simply jump off the rocks into the sea.

In the village of *Suđurad* you can gain a sense of the island's former glory when you look at the restored 16th-century *Country Residence* of the Stjepović-Skočibuha family. Unfortunately, the villa can only be visited as part of an organised excursion from Dubrovnik. If you miss out, then you can console yourself with freshly caught fish and charming service at *Tri Sestre (May–Sept | Suđurad 1C | tel. 020 758 087 | €€€)*.

A trip on the island bus service or a one-hour walk will take you to *Šipanska Luka*, which lies in a deep cove and is centred on an attractive park surrounded by cafés. Here, the restaurant *Kod Marka (May–Sept | tel. 020 75 80 07 | €€€)* is particularly recommended. The chef won't tell you exactly what is on the menu, but it will be fresh and delicious. The *Hotel Šipan (hotelsipan.com)* rents out kayaks and mountain bikes. *L7*

Šipan is popular with day trippers

CAVTAT

M8 **This small town (pop. 2,100), just a short distance from Dubrovnik, achieves an excellent balance between the modern and the traditional. Super-yachts moor along the shoreline, but *kolo* dancing and *klapa* singing are still performed in the local bars. The bay, with its attractive beaches, is popular with local artists.**

A Roman settlement was here as early as the third century BCE, and archaeologists believe that ancient Greeks had already settled on this cove prior to that. However, this Greek city (Epidaurus) disappeared amid the chaos of the migration period during the seventh century CE when its inhabitants fled to an island around 20km to the north, which became the centre of the city republic of Ragusa – later Dubrovnik. Cavtat was resettled from Ragusa during the 14th and 15th centuries, so it's no surprise that the town is reminiscent of its bigger sister.

The northern arm of Cavtat bay – the *Rat peninsula* – is shaped like a lobster claw reaching far out to sea. Its thick Mediterranean vegetation invites visitors to stroll in the shade of pines and cypresses and to bathe at one of its many enchanting coves. On the highest point of the island, the peak of *Sv. Rok*, you will find the city cemetery. Here, decorative gravestones from across the ages are piled against each other around the distinctive *Račić Mausoleum* (see p. 117).

Moor your yacht and step straight onto Cavtat's palm-lined promenade

SIGHTSEEING

OLD TOWN

Cavtat's old town extends uphill from the palm-fronted promenade of the Riva. The parish church of Sv. Nikola overlooks the sea, while its precious treasures are preserved next door in the *Pinacoteca (June–Oct Mon–Sat 10am–1pm, 4–7pm | about 1.50 euros)*. A few steps further on is the *Rector's Palace (Knežev dvor)* with its elegant blend of Gothic and Renaissance architectural features – a miniature copy of the Dubrovnik original. It houses a collection belonging to local intellectual *Baltazar Bogišić (Mon–Sat 9.30am–1.30pm,* admission about 3.50 euros). It combines archaeological finds and art, including the colourful *Carnival in Cavtat* by local art nouveau artist Vlaho Bukovac (1885-1922). Carnival is still celebrated here 100 years later. You can learn more about this painter in his house, the *Kuča Bukovac (Mon–Sat 9am–6pm, Sun 9am–2pm | about 4 euros | Bukovčeva 5 | kuca-bukovac.hr)*. With its original furnishings and ornamental garden hidden behind high walls, the house provides a vivid insight into the bourgeois lifestyle of that time. At the end of the promenade the church and monastery of *Gospe od snijega* are a very peaceful place to sit.

RAČIĆ MAUSOLEUM

The white marble mausoleum of the Račić family perched high over Cavtat is supposed to symbolise birth, life and death, and was created in 1922 by the Croatian master sculptor Ivan Meštrović for a shipping dynasty from Dubrovnik. Based on an ancient temple and watched over by caryatids, this monumental tomb dominates the city cemetery. *Mon–Sat 10am–5pm | about 1.50 euros | ⏲ 15 mins*

EATING & DRINKING

BUGENVILA

The elegant dishes served at the Riva restaurant could be described as works of art. If you're willing to dig deep into your pocket, the tasting menu is definitely worth trying. *Obala Dr A Starčevića 9 | tel. 020 479 949 | bugenvila.eu | €€€*

KONOBA KOLONA

Anyone for swordfish carpaccio, shellfish *buzara* or aubergine tartare? Traditional Dalmatian cuisine is enriched with contemporary touches, and everything is freshly caught by the chef himself. *Put Tihe 2 | tel. 020 478 269 | €€*

ROKOTIN

If you're tired of bad food at the beach, this is your chance to get something much better. Try the grilled seafood dishes and home-made cakes on the raised terrace which has amazing views of the bay. *Ključice b.b. | tel. 020 478 324 | €€*

INSIDER TIP
Tuna on the terrace

SPORT & ACTIVITIES

One of the best diving experiences around is the freight of a sunken Greek trading ship! Its amphorae are protected from theft by a cage but the instructors from *Epidaurum diving centre (Šetalište Žal | beim Hotel Epidaurum | tel. 020 471 386 | epidaurum.com)* have a key and will let you get very close.

BEACHES

The popular beach of *Kamen mali* on the Rat peninsula (10 minutes' walk from the old town) is an idyllic rocky cove with a small, charming bar. However, Pasjača beach – located 13km to the southeast by the village of Popovići – is still a relative secret. Set on a fine shingle cove, it nestles at the foot of a sheer 250m cliff.

NIGHTLIFE

Colourful cocktails and dancing are on offer from many bars on the Riva. See the sun set from the sofas at *Eve Lounge Bar (Šetaliste Zal 2)*. *Beach Bar Cool (Put Tihe 24)* has guest DJs every weekend and the wooden terrace at *Beach Bar Little Star (Kupalište Kamen Mali)* means you can dive straight into the water.

KAMEN MALI

This beach bar is the place to be for drinks and sushi on the Riva, and music plays into the small hours. *Daily 8am–1am | Obala Dr A Starčevića 16*

AROUND CAVTAT

🔢 ĐUROVIĆA CAVE

7km from Cavtat/ 10 mins by car

If you arrive at Čilipi airport, you can continue your descent underground. There is – you see – a natural wonder under the runway. The "Sky Cellar" cave is not only full of stalactites but also houses a museum on local wines from the Konavle region. *Closed for renovation at the time of writing but due to reopen soon | tel. 020 773 331 | short.travel/kkd14 | 🗺 M8*

🔢 ČILIPI & THE KONAVLE VALLEY

8km from Cavtat / 11mins by car

Čilipi is the main village in the *Konavle Valley*, which extends 25km to the south of Cavtat, becoming progressively narrower. Sheltered on its eastern flank by the Sniježnica mountain range (up to 1,234m), the valley is richly fertile and is an important agricultural area in the otherwise sparse karst landscapes of South Dalmatia. That is why the occupation of the valley by Serbian and Montenegrin troops in 1991–2 during the Yugoslav War had such dramatic consequences. The area was devastated and the majority of its 10,000 inhabitants fled to Dubrovnik. Today, however, the region has recovered, as can be seen from the many newly built detached homes.

There are two main attractions in Čilipi. Every Sunday from Easter until October at around 11.15am (at the

end of the weekly church service) the local folklore society *Lindo* performs traditional songs and dances from the Konavle region in front of the church *(about 6 euros including admission to the museum)*. There is also a small market selling handicrafts, including attractive embroidery. These embroideries adorning traditional dress, household goods and bags are a topic of the interesting exhibition at the ethnographic museum *(Zavičajni muzej Konavla | Tue–Sat 9am–4pm, Sun 9am–1pm | about 3.50 euros | Beroje 49)*. You can then round off your trip into the rural hinterland with a hearty meal at the restaurant *Vinica*

Evening by the sea on Cavtat's beach which stretches along the coastline

(Pridvorje | tel. 099 215 2459 | konobavinica.com | €). You will need to book in advance to enjoy the *peka*-cooked lamb, but the other grilled meat and fish dishes on offer are also superb. ▦ *M8*

17 SOKOL FORTRESS
25km / 29 mins from Cavtat

Southeast of Čilipi, the impressive 14th-century fortress of *Sokol grad* (Falcon town) appears to emerge from the rocks around it. Built on the remains of Illyrian and Roman sites, it was the largest fort at the time of the Dubrovnik Republic and of strategic importance because of its position on a mountain pass. From up here, the whole of Konavle stretches out beneath you. Be particularly careful on the steep steps! *(Dunave | April/May 10am–5pm, May–Oct 10am–7pm, Nov 10am–4pm | about 6 euros)*. ▦ *M 8*

INSIDER TIP
Bird's-eye view

Five minutes' drive from here will take you to Sv. Barbara church in Dubravka and its medieval grave-stones or *stećci*. These are now protected by UNESCO but the infra-structure to visit them (by which we mean toilets) has not yet been built.

DISCOVERY TOURS

Want to get under the skin of the region? Then our discovery tours are the ideal guide – they provide advice on which sights to visit, tips on where to stop for that perfect holiday snap, a choice of the best places to eat and drink, and suggestions for fun activities.

❶ VIS'S HIDDEN TREASURES

➤ Get on your bike and explore an idyllic island
➤ Discover Tito's top-secret cave
➤ Beautiful bays and steep cliffs

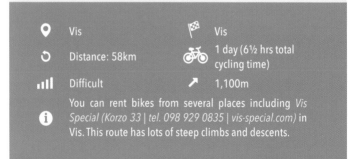

📍	Vis	🏁	Vis
↻	Distance: 58km	🚲	1 day (6½ hrs total cycling time)
📶	Difficult	↗	1,100m

ℹ️ You can rent bikes from several places including *Vis Special (Korzo 33 | tel. 098 929 0835 | vis-special.com)* in Vis. This route has lots of steep climbs and descents.

Split Harbour

UPS & DOWNS

Start off from the town of ① Vis ➤ p. 85. *The first 6km follows route 117 climbing steadily to the west.* Cross through a valley framed by mountain ranges and go past the pre-Romanesque church of Sv. Mihovil, which marks the route's highest point at 385m. After that, *a sometimes steeply winding road leads down to the sea at Komiža* ➤ p. 86. At this point, you've already more than earned an iced coffee at the café ② Fabrika *(Riva Sv. Mikule).*

Ride 500m back uphill on route 117 until the road branches off to the southeast and goes around Hum, the highest mountain on the island (587m). *About 7km later,* signs in Podšpilje point the way to Tito's Cave. From here, *the route to the cave entrance heads north for 700m to the junction at Žena Glava and then another 600m to the west.* In the hamlet of Borovik, you will spot the steps that lead to ③ Titova špilja (Tito's Cave). The partisan leader Josip Broz Tito set up his military HQ here during the last months of the Second World War. After exploring the cave on your own, *return to the junction and cycle a few metres straight on* before stopping for lunch at ④ Konoba Pol Murvu *(tel. 021 715 117 | €–€€)* in the village of Žena Glava.

① Vis	
10km	1hr 10 mins
② Fabrika	
11km	2hrs
③ Titova špilja	
2km	17mins
④ Konoba Pol Murvu	
6km	50mins

GREEN & SILVER TREASURES

Head back to route 117 and cycle along the coast to the east. Near the village of Plisko Polje, 4km from Podšpilje, turn towards Marinje Zemlje, 1.5km further to the southwest, then walk steeply downhill *for approx. 20 minutes to* ⑤ Uvala Stiniva, a magical bay secluded behind the rocks with only a narrow gap out to the sea. Enjoy a well-earned dip!

INSIDER TIP
Sensational swimming

⑤ **Uvala Stiniva**
7.5km   25mins

Return to Plisko Polje and follow the main road for 1.5km to the east and then turn right onto the road that leads downhill to ⑥ Rukavac. In this small village with its green bay, embark on a boat trip to ⑦ Ravnik Island with its lesser known, but still very beautiful Green Cave (Zelena špilja), which turns turquoise when the sun shines on it. Once you're back on Vis, check out another lovely beach, ⑧ Uvala Srebrna (Silver Bay), 250m west of Rukavac.

⑥ **Rukavac**
15km   20mins by boat

⑦ **Ravnik Island**
2.5km
35mins boat,10mins road

⑧ **Uvala Srebrna**
7.5km   35mins

A RARE SANDY BEACH

Back in Podstražje, follow the road for 5km until a dirt track branches off to the right. Follow this for another 2.5km to ⑨ Stončica Bay. A footpath leads from the car

⑨ **Stončica Bay**

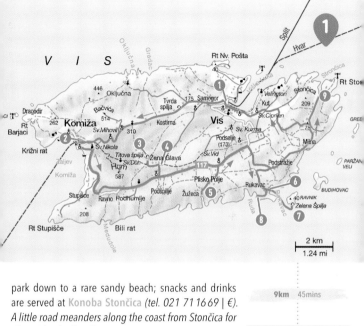

park down to a rare sandy beach; snacks and drinks are served at Konoba Stončica *(tel. 021 71 16 69 | €). A little road meanders along the coast from Stončica for about 9km back to* ❶ Vis*.*

9km   45mins

❶ Vis

You can walk to Stiniva Bay – or arrive by boat

❷ FROM ZADAR TO INLAND WONDERS

➤ Climbing cliffs with incredible views
➤ Sensational swimming under a waterfall
➤ Meandering through millennia of history

📍 Zadar

🏁 Šibenik

→ Distance: 490km

🚗 5 days (7 hrs total driving time)

ℹ Kit list: walking shoes, tent, swimming costume, food for the trip to Plitvice (there are very few shops). Set off as early as possible to ❻ **Plitvice Lakes National Park**, thus avoiding the coach trips; the gates open at 7am.

DAY 1

❶ **Zadar**

21km   25mins

❷ **Sv. Križ**

6km   12mins

❸ **Kraljičina plaža**

52km   60mins

❹ **Starigrad-Paklenica**

16km   21mins

❺ **Camp Vrata Velebita**

18km   25mins

DAY 2

❻ **Paklenica National Park**

165km   2hrs

FROM THE MUSIC OF THE WAVES TO A MUD BATH

In ❶ Zadar ➤ p. 42 , you can enjoy a "maritime concert" at the Sea Organ ➤ p. 44 and check out Sv. Donat ➤ p. 43 before driving *north on route 306*. When you get to Nin (Km16), visit ❷ Sv. Križ, "the world's smallest cathedral". Afterwards have a dip in the ❸ Kraljičina plaža before *heading southeast for 17km to the junction with the E65. Take the Adriatic Highway towards Rijeka. The route over the Maslenica Bridge will bring you to* ❹ Starigrad-Paklenica and the national park. Pitch your tent at ❺ Camp Vrata Velebita *(vratavelebita.com)*, to the north of Starigrad.

DISCOVER YOUR INNER CHAMOIS

Early the next morning, *head back to Starigrad to get to the main entrance of the* ❻ Paklenica National Park ➤ p. 48, a true hiking and climbing paradise. Don't miss out on watching the free climbers who hang like colourful spiders on the rocky walls of the two canyons. There are walls here for climbers of all levels. Hike for a couple of hours along the mix of easy and more challenging climbing trails through the Velika Paklenica canyon, past several mills to the little lodge of Lugarnica

(June–Sept, daily 10.30am–4.30pm), which serves simple food and drinks. Walk back to the entrance via the same route and camp for another night at Vrata Velebita.

TURQUOISE LAKES

To get to your next destination, *drive along the E65 back towards the Maslenica Bridge and turn left before the bridge onto the toll road A1 heading to Karlovac and Zagreb. After 48km, take exit 13 (Gornja Ploča).* National road D1 crosses over the rocky landscape of Karjina via Udbina and Korenica. *After driving 50km,* you will be astounded by the lush green vegetation at the main entrance to the 200-km² area of the ❼ Plitvice Lakes National Park ➤ p.48, where crashing waterfalls connect the 16 lakes. On the marked circular route, you will walk for two hours along the upper lakes and then

DAY 3

❼ Plitvice Lakes National Park

187km 2hrs

Awe-inspiring waterfalls in the Plitvice Lakes National Park

another two hours along the lower ones. Stop for coffee at the bistro Kozjačka Draga on Lake Kozjak. Afterwards, rest your head for the night at Hotel Jezero *(jezero-hotel-plitvice-lakes.hotel-ds.com)* near the main entrance to the park.

THE BEST NATURAL SHOWER

The next morning, follow the same route back on the B1, but drive further past Gračac (67km) towards Knin (about another 50km), where you will come to the River Krka. A 45km stretch of the river between Kninsko Polje and Skradin has been declared a conservation area. *Your route mainly follows the river on roads 59 (34km) and 56 (16km) to Skradin in order to access the* ❽ Krka National Park ➤ p. 62. Stroll along the wooden walkways to watch the river cascade down to the valley below. Skradinski buk is the name of the most famous waterfall and is a great place to have a swim. Put on your swimsuit and take a shower under the foaming water. A small museum with a simple eatery displays a collection of local customs and traditional dress. *Return to Skradin* where the best place to stay is the mid-range hotel ❾ Skradinski buk *(skradinskibuk.hr).*

DAY 4

❽ **Krka National Park**

7km 50mins

❾ **Skradinski buk**

20km 25mins

Enjoy a bit of traditional Dalmatia in Amadria Park's recreated village

OLD ARCHITECTURE, MODERN FESTIVAL

After breakfast, *follow the D56 to the southeast and then D33 to the southwest* to get back to the little city of ⑩ Šibenik ➤ p. 58. After so many days in the wilderness, the old town centre with its unusual Renaissance and Baroque buildings makes for a nice change. The wine bar Vino i Ino ➤ p. 60 is an architectural and culinary delight. And by the end of your tour you will have earned a lengthy stay at one of the beach resort hotels in the Amadria Park *(amadriapark.com)* which sits on a pretty peninsula.

DAY 5

⑩ Šibenik

❸ VINEYARDS & OLIVE GROVES

➤ Find out how the very best olive oil is produced
➤ Ride a mountain bike through the vineyards
➤ Enjoy a glass of red with the winemaker

📍 Split

🏁 Ston
4 days (4 hrs total driving time)

➡ Distance: 210km 🚗

ℹ Don't forget to bring your swimming costume. Book a wine and bike tour with Mario Bartulović *(tours@bartul. com)* well in advance!

DAY 1
❶ Split
79km 3.5hrs

❷ Uljara Zlokić
21km 24mins

❸ Aminess Lume Hotel
5km 7mins

DAY 2

OLIVE GREEN IS THE COLOUR FOR THIS TOUR

Set off from ❶ Split ➤ p. 71 at around 10am for this tour of culinary treats. *Car ferry 604* – run by *Jadrolinija (jadrolinija.hr)* – takes only three hours for the crossing to Vela Luka on Korčula. The island's wines and oils used to be exported from here. The olive oils made by ❷ Uljara Zlokić *(Mon–Fri 10am–noon, 6–8pm | Ulica 6. br. 13 | tel. 098 929 5073 | uljarazlokic.com)* are internationally acclaimed. There is an exhibition of machinery and plenty of opportunities to try the oils. *Afterwards, drive through olive groves on route 118 heading eastward and, at the junction, take the Ulica 1 south to Blato. From here, head towards Prizba on the southern coast.* Enjoy the beautiful vistas as you *drive along the coastal road to the east for 8km to Brna.* Tiny offshore islands are dotted between deep, sheltered bays. Spend the night in *Brna* at the ❸ Aminess Lume Hotel *(aminess. com)*.

AN IDYLLIC MINI DUBROVNIK

Your route heads inland the next day, *going northeast to Smokvica*, the major winegrowing area for the Pošip and Rukatac grape varieties that produce light and fresh white wines. Try the excellent examples made by the ❹ Toreta winery *(Smokvica 165 | tel. 020 83 21 00). The next 16km on route 118 to Pupnat are quite an adventure!* The sometimes dizzying stretch of road meanders above the coast to ❺ Pupnatska Luka (11km). You simply must go for a swim here in one of the prettiest bays on Korčula. Drive a few kilometres further and treat yourself to a hearty lunch of home-grown food in ❻ Pupnat at the Konoba Mate *(Pupnat 28 | tel. 020 717 109 | €€)*, located right next to the church and surrounded by grapevines. *After another 11km on the D118, you will arrive in the picturesque town of* ❼ Korčula ➤ p. 99, where you should plan to spend the second night. Make sure you visit the cathedral before checking into the Korčula De La Ville *(korcula-hotels.com)*, a modern hotel on the edge of the old town with great views of the sea.

TAKE A FERRY TO MORE VINEYARDS

The next morning, *hop aboard the ferry to Orebić on the Pelješac peninsula.* It is a short crossing, but it offers the most beautiful view of Korčula's old town. ❽ Orebić ➤ p. 96 itself is an old seafaring town, but as soon as you *drive inland along route 414 towards Donja Banda and cross over the hills*, there are vineyards everywhere. As the soil is barren and rocky, the vines are planted on small fields surrounded by high drystone walls to protect them from the wind. About *2km after Donja Banda, you will come to the tiny village of* Prizdrina (pop. 20) with its old stone houses. The famous vintner Mario Bartulović will let you look over his shoulder as he works at ❾ Bartulović Winery *(4 rooms, 1 bungalow | tel. 020 742 506 | vinarijabartulovic.hr | €€)*. Using the southern Dalmatian grape variety of *Plavac mali,* he produces excellent red wines sold under the brand *Bartul.* As Mario himself likes to keep fit, he will take overnight guests on *wine tours by mountain bike (from about 67 euros per person | tours@bartul.com).* You will cycle along paths and through vineyards to the neighbouring wineries to taste the characteristic Pelješac wines.

❹ **Toreta**
11km   15mins

❺ **Pupnatska Luka**
6km   6mins

❻ **Pupnat**
11km   13mins

❼ **Korčula**
8km   50mins incl. ferry

DAY 3

❽ **Orebić**
16km   18mins

❾ **Bartulović Winery**
5km   8mins

DAY 4	
⑩ **Potomje**	
9km　16mins	
⑪ **Grgić Vina**	
7km　13mins	
⑫ **Vina Skaramuča**	
8km　9mins	
⑬ **Taverna Domanoeta**	
2km　4mins	
⑭ **Drače**	
28km　28mins	
⑮ **Ston**	

AT THE HEART OF THE WINE REGION

The next day, *drive a few kilometres southeast on route 414* to the village of ⑩ Potomje at the heart of the *Dingač* region. Pass through the narrow, slightly scary tunnel carved into the rock by the winemakers *to get to the southern coast*, where the special grape variety of *Plavac mali* ripens on the steep slopes. The *narrow road snakes along the terraced vineyards to the east for 8km to Trstenik*. The village is home to the winery of ⑪ Grgić Vina *(tel. 020 74 80 90 | grgic-vina.com)*, which belongs to the most famous of the Pelješac winemakers, Mike Grgich. He made his fortune and a name for himself in California before returning to his homeland where he began to make internationally acclaimed *Dingač* wines.

MUSSELS & OILS WITH LOCAL WINES

Cross over the steep mountain ridge for 2km back to the north and then take route 414 for 5km to the west to get to Pijavičino. This is where Ivo Skaramuča, with his estate ⑫ Vina Skaramuča *(tel. 098 73 75 42 | dingac-skaramuca.hr),* is hoping to become Pelješac's best vintner. Unlike others, he ages his *Dingač* wines in oak barrels and the little detour to his vineyard is definitely worthwhile. *Now head eastwards along route 414 until you come to Janjina (approx. 9km)* and the ⑬ Taverna Domanoeta *(Janjina 51 | tel. 020 741 406 | €)*. The taverna belongs to a charming Croatian/Italian couple who will do their utmost to give you a good time (and fill you up). *Another 2km on route 414 will bring you to the northern coast near* ⑭ Drače, where mussels and oysters are farmed in the shallow bay. The final stop on the tour is ⑮ Ston ➤ p. 97, which lies *30km to the southeast on route 414*. Not only does Vinarija Miloš *(Ponikve 15 | tel. 020 753 098 | milos.hr)* produce a full-bodied *Plavac Stagnum,* but it has also begun to make organic olive oil and tea. *Oblica* and *Pastrica* are the names of the local olive varieties that lend Frano Miloš's oil its fine, fruity note. It even seems to have a taste of the fragrant maquis shrubland so characteristic of Pelješac.

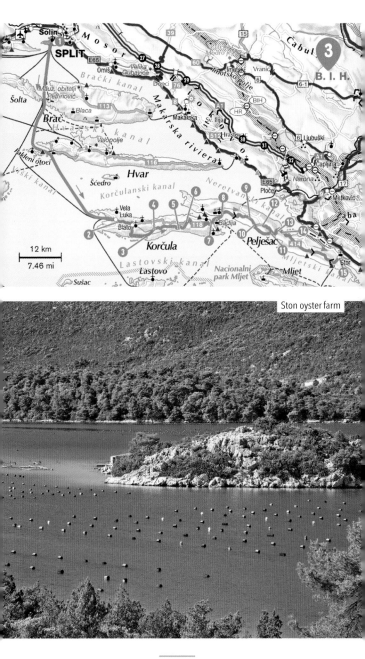

Ston oyster farm

GOOD TO KNOW
HOLIDAY BASICS

ARRIVAL

BEFORE YOU GO

For details of Croatian National Tourist Offices around the world, go to *visit-croatia.co.uk/croatian-tourist-offices*. The main website for the Croatian National Tourist Board is *www.croatia.hr*. Also useful is *findcroatia.com*

GETTING THERE
AIR

There are flights from all over the UK to all the Dalmatian (and other Croatian) airports. There are also flights to Croatia from Ireland. Inland flights are available from Zagreb to Zadar, Split and Dubrovnik.

CAR

The A1 motorway from Zagreb currently ends in Ploče, although an extension to Dubrovnik is under construction. Note that tolls are charged on all Croatia's motorways. It is not worth trying to get out of these fees as the motorways are much quicker than alternative routes. The only exception may be during summer if there is very heavy traffic (especially on Saturdays).

INSIDER TIP
Don't count the pennies

If you travel from Croatia's north, you no longer have to cross Bosnian territory at Neum (with all the usual passport and customs checks) in order to continue south to Dubrovnik. The Pelješac Bridge between Komarma and the peninsula now makes it possible to get to Dubrovnik exclusively on Croatian soil.

COACH

Coaches to Zagreb, Rijeka and Split depart from London and many continental European towns. From there

View over Korčula

you can find connections to Croatia's very well-developed public bus network. *eurolines.com, croatiabus.hr*

FERRY

An attractive alternative to driving down the tricky coastal road to southern Dalmatia is to take the car ferry from Italy. The main routes are: Bari–Dubrovnik (up to six times a week); Ancona–Split (daily); Ancona–Stari Grad/Hvar (once a week, July/August twice a week); and Ancona–Zadar (daily). Compare prices on *direct ferries.com* and book well in advance.

RAIL

EuroCity trains to Zagreb depart from Germany and Austria. Some trains have through coaches to Rijeka during the summer months. National trains run to Zadar, Šibenik and Split. Use www. seat61.com/Croatia.htm to research the best connections from the UK.

GETTING IN

For a maximum stay of 90 days UK (and US) citizens will need a passport that is valid for the duration of their stay and six months thereafter.

CLIMATE & WHEN TO GO

The peak season is in July and August (especially the first two weeks of August) when prices are at their highest and hotel and restaurant availability is at its lowest. It is best to avoid tourist hotspots like the Plitvice Lakes and Dubrovnik in this period or else time your trip very carefully.

The summers tend to be sunny and warm during the day, while the nights are refreshingly cooler. From time to time black clouds build up and there's an afternoon thunderstorm. Since the Adriatic is not particularly deep, the sea quickly warms up to 20°C in the early summer, and up to 26°C in August. The best time to go is mid-May to the end of June, when the gorse is flowering, and in September, when the summer heat is not so intense but the Adriatic is still pleasantly warm. During the late summer and autumn months, the cold katabatic Bora wind can bring changes in the weather and choppy seas.

GETTING AROUND

BOAT

Regional ferry connections from the mainland to the islands are largely operated by the national shipping company *Jadrolinija (jadrolinija.hr)*, which runs connections on fast catamarans (passengers only) as well as on car ferries. Bigger boats will offer more gastronomic and entertainment services (the biggest have chapels and playrooms). Most ferries have WiFi but the quality can vary horribly. It is not possible to reserve for specific services. For that reason, drivers should queue up well before the ship's departure; in peak season two to three hours depending on the route.

Although it is becoming ever more popular, island hopping is a bit trickier here than in Greece. There are relatively few ferries between the islands and you often have to go back to the mainland to get to your destination. These complications can eat up your holiday, so if you do decide to island hop, limit the number of stops.

BUS

The local bus network is good and covers all the smaller towns along the coast and also on the islands. Private companies are a bit more expensive but normally come with WiFi and are a bit more comfortable. For timetables, see *croatiabus.hr*. The journey from Split to Dubrovnik costs about 17 euros, for example.

CAR

Speed limits are 50kmh in towns, 90kmh outside towns, 110kmh on some A-roads and dual carriageways and 130kmh on motorways. Towing vehicles outside towns are restricted to 80kmh. Drivers under 24 have to drive 10 kmh slower (except in towns and villages). The legal alcohol limit is 50mg per 100ml but there is zero tolerance for under 24s. During the winter months (last Sunday in October until last Sunday in March) you must switch on your headlights (dipped) at all times (even during the day). There are not many car parks in the older parts of cities and the ones that do exist are expensive.

Croatia has a well-developed network of petrol stations; all types of fuel are available at EU quality. The Croatian breakdown service HAK is staffed around the clock: *tel. 1987*. It also runs an app: *Croatia-traffic-info*.

CAR HIRE

International and local car rental places can be found in every sizeable resort and town. The requirements for renting a vehicle are not the same everywhere. In most cases you need to be at least 21

FESTIVALS & EVENTS
ALL YEAR ROUND

FEBRUARY
St Blaise's Day (Sv. Vlaho) (Dubrovnik): Processions and music in honour of the city's patron saint.

JUNE/JULY
☻ *International Children's Festival* (Šibenik): Music, games, acrobatics and plays. *mdf-sibenik.com*

JULY
Dubrovnik Summer Festival Six weeks of music, opera and theatre. *dubrovnik-festival.hr*
Moreška (Korčula): Jousting matches and a unique sword dance. *visitkorcula.net/moreska.html*
Regius (Šibenik): Alt-rock festival with local bands. *regius-festival.com*
Soundwave (Tisno): Reggae and hip hop in a relaxed beach location. *soundwavecroatiacom*
Ultra (Split): Europe's most famous electro festival. *ultraeurope.com*
🏴 *Klapa Festival* (Omiš): Omiš plays host to Croatia's choirs as they compete to be the best in the country. *fdk.hr/festival*

JULY/AUGUST
Musical Evenings in Sv. Donat (Zadar): Classical concerts with extraordinary acoustics. *donat-festival.com*
Summer Carnival Held in lots of coastal resorts including Makarska, Senj and Bol.
Split Summer Open-air theatre, opera and ballet. *splitsko-ljeto.hr*

AUGUST
Diocletian' Days (Split): Togas and chariots take Split back to Roman times.
Saljske užance (Sali): Local festival with donkey races, fishermen's banquets and *klapa* music.
Sinjska alka (Sinj): Three-day festival with a traditional knights' tournament. *alka.hr*
Night of the Pirates (Omiš): A spectacular sea battle recounts this pirate town's history.

and have had two years' driving experience. A medium-sized car will cost around 30 euros a day. Use online comparison sites to get the best prices.

EMERGENCIES

EMBASSIES
UK EMBASSY
Ivana Lučića 4 | Zagreb | tel. 385 1 600 9100 | gov.uk/world/organisations/british-embassy-zagreb

US EMBASSY
Ulica Thomasa Jeffersona 2 | Zagreb | tel. 385 1 661 2200 | usembassy.gov/croatia

CANADIAN EMBASSY
Prilaz Gjure Dezelica 4 | Zagreb | tel. 385 1 488 1200 | croatia.gc.ca

AUSTRALIAN EMBASSY
Centar Kaptol, 3rd floor Nova Ves 11 | Zagreb | tel. 385 1 489 1200 | croatia.embassy.gov.au

EMERGENCY CALLS
In an emergency dial the free number 112, which also has English-speaking operators. To call Maritime Search and Rescue (MRCC RIJEKA), dial 195.

HEALTH
There are no special health risks in Dalmatia but it is important to take good precautions against the sun. Bring a cooling gel to treat sunburns and mosquito bites as well as beach shoes to provide protection against sharp rocks and sea urchins. Hikers visiting the islands should take proper boots that have a good ankle support. A higher boot is also advisable because of the many snakes, some of which are venomous.

On the mainland and the larger islands there are pharmacies as well as doctors who speak English. Make sure you have good travel insurance.

SAFETY
Don't leave valuables unattended on the beach. If you need to, use a prop (like a large suncream bottle) to hide them! Don't lose sight of your belongings in crowded places either.

Campfires and late-night cigarettes out in the wild may contribute to your idea of a good holiday but in the extremely dry summer months, they can also be responsible for terrible forest fires. Make sure you use torches and only smoke in safe places.

Never go out on the sea during the Bora winds, as any local sailor will tell you. Just being outside in these winds can be dangerous. But if you come to Dalmatia in the summer, you should be OK: the Bora tends to crash through in late autumn.

ESSENTIALS

BEACHES
Most beaches are pebbly, but there are a few sandy ones. Public beaches normally have all mod cons. A shower will cost you a few cents. Access to beaches is free but car parks generally

charge a fee. There is normally a set swimming area outside of which you risk of getting too close to boats.

CAMPING

Camping and caravanning are not allowed outside designated sites. Croatia has modernized most of its sites to conform to enhanced international standards. In some places you can also rent apartments and bungalows. If large sites with more than a thousand pitches are not your thing, you will also find smaller ones. Naturists will appreciate the high standards in the naturist camps. A list and descriptions of the campsites can be found at *camping.hr.*

CUSTOMS

If travelling within the EU, there are very few strict customs rules. However, if travelling from the UK and other non-EU countries you will need to check your allowances before bringing things in or out of the country.

DRINKING WATER

Tap water is drinkable almost everywhere in Dalmatia, but it is often heavily chlorinated. Bottled mineral water is tastier and also inexpensive.

INFORMATION

Tourist information offices *(Turistička zajednica)* can help with travel arrangements and city maps etc. In the high season, they are open all day; at other times of year some are only open in the morning (or else take a long lunch break). Many private travel agencies specialise in booking accommodation as well as excursions. The addresses and websites of all the tourism offices can be found at *croatia. hr* under the relevant destinations.

HOW MUCH DOES IT COST

Coffee	*1.50-2 euros for an espresso in a touristy spot*
Ice cream	*2 euros for two scoops*
Snacks	*1.50 euros for a piece of burek (stuffed pastry)*
Pizza	*6-9 euros in a restaurant*
Fuel	*1.40 euros for 1 litre super unleaded*
Deckchair	*4-8 euros for a day's rental*

MARINAS & YACHTING

All marinas include electricity and water (including waste) in their prices, some will offer other services too. Many are run by ACI Marinas. You can book online or via an app: *aci-marinas. com.* To call a lifeboat/Maritime Search and Rescue *(MRCC RIJEKA),* dial 195.

MONEY

On 1 January 2023 Croatia adopted the euro and the kuna ceased to be the country's official currency. Note that euro prices given in this guidebook are converted from kuna prices and should be treated as estimates only; actual prices are likely to be a bit higher.

Send a postcard from the Makarska Riviera

In centres like Dubrovnik and Hvar prices are much higher than the average place on the coast. Cards are accepted in the larger towns but it is also worth carrying some cash, especially on the islands. You generally pay in cash in restaurants. Most banks are open Monday–Friday 7am–7pm, Saturday 7am–1pm. There are cash machines everywhere (check their fees).

OPENING TIMES

Most restaurants are open from noon until the evening during the main season. Only very few smarter places can afford restricted opening times or even a day off. During the low season, however, only some of the hotels, restaurants and shops are open in the holiday resorts.

Museum opening times also vary throughout the year and you are advised to enquire on the spot at the local tourist information office.

POST

Opening times of post offices (pošta) are not the same everywhere, but they are usually open Monday–Friday 7am–7pm, Saturday 8am–1pm. The cost of sending a postcard to another country is less than 1 euro.

PUBLIC HOLIDAYS

1 Jan	New Year's Day
6 Jan	Epiphany
March/April	Easter
1 May	International Labour Day
30 May	Statehood Day
May/June	Corpus Christi
22 June	Anti-Fascist Struggle Day
5 Aug	Victory Day
15 Aug	Feast of the Assumption
8 Oct	Independence Day
1 Nov	All Souls' Day
25/26 Dec	Christmas

SMOKING

Smoking is not allowed in any public building, restaurant or hotel in Dalmatia. Anyone disregarding this can expect to pay stiff fines.

TELEPHONE & WIFI

How much you pay for using your phone will depend on your deal at home. Many of the bigger cities have free WiFi in public places.

The country code for Croatia is 00385. When making a call from Croatia, dial 0044 for the UK; 00353 for Ireland; 001 for the US and Canada; 0061 for Australia; then dial the local code without "0" and then the individual number.

TIPPING

Good service in a restaurant should be rewarded with around 10–15 percent of the bill. Hotel staff also expect a small gesture.

WEATHER IN SPLIT

High season
Low season

	JAN	FEB	MARCH	APRIL	MAY	JUNE	JULY	AUG	SEPT	OCT	NOV	DEC
Daytime temperature	10°	11°	14°	18°	22°	27°	31°	31°	26°	21°	16°	11°
Night-time temperatures	5°	5°	7°	10°	14°	18°	21°	20°	17°	14°	11°	6°
Hours of sunshine per day	4	5	6	7	9	10	12	11	8	6	4	3
Rainy days per month	9	8	8	7	7	6	4	3	6	8	11	12
Sea temperature in °C	13	12	13	14	17	21	23	24	22	19	16	14

☀ Hours of sunshine per day   🌂 Rainy days per month   ≈ Sea temperature in °C

WORDS & PHRASES
IN CROATIAN

SMALLTALK

yes/no/maybe	da/ne/možda
please/thank you	molim/hvala
Excuse me (informal/formal)	Oprosti!/Oprostite!
Good morning/good afternoon/ goodnight!	Dobro jutro!/Dobar dan!/Laku noć!
Hello/bye/goodbye!	Bok! (Ćao!; Halo!)/Ćao!/Doviđenja!
My name is ...	Zovem se ...
What is your name? (formal/informal)	Kako se zovete? Kako se zoveš?
I come from ...	Dolazim iz ...
E-mail address	E-mail adresa
May I ...?/Pardon?	Smijem li ...?/Molim?
I (don't) like this	To mi se (ne) sviđa.
good/bad	dobro/loše
I would like.../Do you have ... ?	Htio (f: Htjela) bih .../Imate li ...?
Do you speak English? (formal/ informal)	Govorite li engleski?/Govoriš li engleski?

SYMBOLS

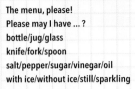

EATING & DRINKING

The menu, please!	Mogu li dobiti jelovnik, molim?
Please may I have ... ?	Mogu li dobiti ...?
bottle/jug/glass	butelju/karafu/čašu
knife/fork/spoon	nož/vilicu/žlicu
salt/pepper/sugar/vinegar/oil	sol/papar/šećer/ocat/ulje
with ice/without ice/still/sparkling	s ledom/bez leda/(ne)gazirana
vegetarian/allergy	vegetarijanac; vegetarijanka/ alergičar; alergičarka
I would like to pay, please	Želio bih platiti, molim.
bill/tip	račun/napojnica
cash/debit card/credit card	gotovina/debitna kartica/ kreditna kartica

MISCELLANEOUS

Where is ...?/Where are ...?	Gdje je ...?/Gdje su ...?
What time is it?	Koliko je sati?
today/tomorrow/yesterday	danas/sutra/jučer
How much is ...?	Koliko košta ...?
Where can I get internet/WiFi?	Gdje mogu naći pristup internetu/ WiFi?
pharmacy/chemist/bakery/market	ljekarna/drogerija/pekarnica/ tržnica
fever/pain/inflammation/injury	temperatura/bolovi/upala/povreda
broken/not working	pokvaren/ne funkcionira
breakdown/garage	nezgoda/radionica
Help/beware/careful!	Upomoć!/Upozorenje!/Oprez!
ban/forbidden/danger/dangerous	zabrana/zabranjeno/opasnost/ opasno
0/1/2/3/4/5/6/7/8/9/10/100/1000	nula/jedan/dva/tri/četiri/pet/ šest/sedam/osam/devet/deset/ sto/tisuću

HOLIDAY VIBES

FOR RELAXATION & CHILLING

FOR BOOKWORMS & FILM BUFFS

📖 BLACK LAMB AND GREY FALCON

Rebecca West, a redoubtable Englishwoman, and her banker husband travelled round Yugoslavia in the 1930s. She recorded her impressions in a fascinating and classic account.

📖 FAREWELL, COWBOY

Written by local Split woman Olja Savičević Ivančevi, this charming but gritty book tells the story of a Western movie being shot near the author's hometown. It may not all be beaches and sun, but it is a great read.

🎥 THE WEEKEND AWAY

Set in Split and produced by Netflix, this 2022 film is high concept and very thrilling. Definitely not a film to watch while getting ready for a night out in Diocletian's city, however.

🎥 SVECENIKOVA DJECA (THE PRIEST'S CHILDREN)

This is a very amusing feature film by the Croatian director Vinko Brešan (2014). It's a comedy about the church, morals, everyday life on an island and... condoms, set on an unnamed island in the Adriatic.

PLAYLIST

◫ ⏮ ⏸ ⏭ 🔊 ————————

0:58

⏸ **DENIS MARIČIĆ** – OČI BOJE LAVANDE
A *klapa* classic which serenades lavender-coloured eyes.

▶ **DJEČACI – DALMACIJA**
A taste of contemporary Split in this ironic and slangy bit of Dalmatian hip hop.

▶ **HLADNO PIVO – ZIMMER FREI**
Punk band *Cold Beer* dream of kicking back in a bar.

▶ **OLIVER DRAGOJEVIĆ – CESARICA**
Written by Gibonni and sung by Dragojević, this is a collaboration between two of the region's biggest stars.

▶ **TOMISLAV IVČIĆ** – VEČERAS JE NAŠA FEŠTA
Dalmatia's unofficial anthem: "this evening it is our party, this evening we will drink wine!"

The holiday soundtrack is available at **Spotify** under **MARCO POLO Croatia**

Or scan the code with the Spotify app

ONLINE

AGROTURIZAM ZADAR
Sustainable tourism is all the rage. This app will help you to find the greenest wine, cheese and oil from across the whole region.

CHASINGTHEDONKEY.COM
This website is full of tips for great food and cool places. It even offers a bit of help with the language.

MAKARSKA RIVIERA BEACHES
The number of stunning beaches on the Makarska Riviera may seem overwhelming at first. This app has the

lowdown on them all so you can pick the best spot for a dip.

SECRET CROATIA.BLOG
Abandoned ruins, forgotten history and hidden spots all over Dalmatia which most tourists never find out about. The best kind of travel blog.

SECRET ZADAR
One of the more unusual apps about travel destinations in Dalmatia, Secret Zadar offers little snippets about the history of the region.

TRAVEL PURSUIT

THE MARCO POLO HOLIDAY QUIZ

Do you know your facts about Dalmatia? Here you can test your knowledge of the little secrets and idiosyncrasies of the region and its people. You will find the correct answers below, with further details on pages 18 to 23 of this guide.

❶ Which wind is said to be responsible for people's bad moods?
a) Bora
b) Maestral
c) Jugo

❷ What is Dalmatia's biggest football club called?
a) Hajduk
b) Dinamo
c) Torcida

❸ What is the name of the architect who designed Sv. Jakov Cathedal in Šibenik?
a) Nikola Firentinac
b) Andrija Aleši
c) Juraj Dalmatinac

❹ What kind of spectacle takes place in Tribunj every year?
a) A competition among the hardest-working olive pickers
b) A bizarre donkey race
c) A loud *klapa* competition

❺ The presence of which form of marine life normally means the sea is very clean?
a) Sea urchins
b) Sea cucumbers
c) Crabs

Pišćena Beach on Hvar

❻ What was Dubrovnik's name when it was an independent city state?
a) Regata
b) Regius
c) Ragusa

❼ What was the innovation used by Dubrovnik's population in the 14th century to protect them against the plague?
a) Hospital
b) Quarantine
c) Vaccination

❽ Which famous figure reputedly made the Croatian cravat a global phenomenon?
a) Napoleon
b) Louis XIV
c) Marco Polo

❾ What is the original meaning of the word *konoba*?
a) Dark cellar
b) Cocktail
c) Large wine barrel

❿ What is the rough top speed that the Bora wind can reach?
a) 118 kmh
b) 170 kmh
c) 200 kmh

⓫ Which instrument is sometimes used to accompany *klapa* choirs?
a) Flute
b) Tamburica
c) Harmonica

⓬ What is the main event at the famous summer festival in Iž?
a) A competition for the best wig
b) A sword dance
c) The election of a "king"

INDEX

WE WANT TO HEAR FROM YOU!

Did you have a great holiday? Is there something on your mind? Whatever it is, let us know! Whether you want to praise the guide, alert us to errors or give us a personal tip – MARCO POLO would be pleased to hear from you. Please contact us by email:

We do everything we can to provide the very latest information for your trip. Nevertheless, despite all of our authors' thorough research, errors can creep in. MARCO POLO does not accept any liability for this.

sales@heartwoodpublishing.co.uk

PICTURE CREDITS

Cover photo: Primošten, Croatia (iStock/rusm)
Photos: N. Čančar (147); DuMont Bildarchiv: H. Madej (20); Getty Images: S. Skafar (12/13), G. van der Knijff (116); Getty Images/robertharding: O. Wintzen (142/143); huber-images: F. Cogoli (45, 46/47, 50, 61), L. Debelkova (38/39, 88), J. Foulkes (front and rear inside cover flap/1, 31, 64/65, 113, 120/121), F. Franco (8, 74), P. Giocoso (114), Gräfenhain (101), J. Huber (6/7, 14/15, 80), Irek (54), S. Kremer (11), D. Pearson (109), J. Pearson (132/133), U. Siebig (126), S. Surac (rear inside cover flap, 49), J. Wlodarczyk (2/3, 58); Laif: P. Hirth (10), G. Standl (27, 30/31); Laif/hemis.fr: D. Delfino (77), B. Gardel (57), J.-F. Mallet (84); Laif/robertharding: M. Williams-Ellis (102), O. Wintzen (144/145); Laif/VU: M. Siragusa (9); Look/age fotostock (90, 119); Look/robertharding (69, 83); mauritius images: R. Hackenberg (97), C. Sanchez Pereyra (87), U. Siebig (62), J. Warburton-Lee (110); mauritius images/Alamy: (35), LatitudeStock (135), N. Marcutti (79), RooM the Agency (125); mauritius images/ClickAlps (122/123); mauritius images/imagebroker: fotosol (24/25); mauritius images/Lumi Images: Romulic/Stojcic (23), D. Secen (32/33); mauritius images/Masterfile: R. I. Lloyd (73, 106); mauritius images/McPHOTO: J. Webeler (52/53); mauritius images/robertharding: B. Pipe (92/93); mauritius images/United Archives (99); picture-alliance/PIXSELL: T. Katic/Halo (19), N. Pavletic (26/27); Shutterstock: Stjepan Tafra (28), Geza Kurka Photo Video (91), xbrchx (131), hurricanehank (138)

4th Edition – fully revised and updated 2023
Worldwide Distribution: Heartwood Publishing Ltd, Bath, United Kingdom
www.heartwoodpublishing.co.uk

Authors: Nina Čančar, Daniela Schetar
Editor: Leonie Neumann
Picture editor: Anja Schlatterer
Cartography: © MAIRDUMONT, Ostfildern (pp. 36–37, 123, 127, 131, pull-out map; © MAIRDUMONT, Ostfildern, using data from OpenStreetMap, licence CC-BY-SA 2.0 (pp. 40–41, 42, 66–67, 70, 94–95, 104–105)
Cover design and pull-out map cover design: bilekjaeger_Kreativagentur with Zukunftswerkstatt, Stuttgart
Page design: Langenstein Communication GmbH, Ludwigsburg

Heartwood Publishing credits:
Translated from the German by John Owen, John Sykes, Susan Jones and Suzanne Kirkbright
Editors: Felicity Laughton, Kate Michell, Sophie Blacksell Jones
Prepress: Summerlane Books, Bath
Printed in India

MARCO POLO AUTHOR
NINA ČANČAR

After spending as much time as possible in the Adriatic as a child, it is perhaps unsurprising that Nina Čančar prefers admiring fish to eating them. Today she finds it hard to leave sunny Dalmatia and happily combines her passion with her profession by working as a tour guide, translator and … travel guide writer in her favourite region.

DOS & DON'TS

HOW TO AVOID SLIP-UPS & BLUNDERS

DON'T MISUNDERSTAND LOUD CONVERSATION

Two locals are wildly gesticulating and shouting at each other? Don't worry, they are probably just suggesting meeting for a coffee. You may think the tone in Croatia is aggressive – they would say it's passionate.

DON'T BATHE WITHOUT SHOES

Dalmatia's amazing beaches don't just attract tourists. Sea urchins lurk all along the coast in the clear water. Their spines are seriously painful so don't forget to wear something on your feet while swimming.

DO SHOW RESPECT IN CHURCHES

Dalmatia is conservative and showing too much flesh in a church does not go down well, nor does wandering around town in a bikini. The latter can cost you 600 euros. Make sure you pack appropriate clothing for your whole holiday … the mountain rescue here has had to assist people who went walking in the mountains in flip flops!

DON'T DRINK THE LOCAL MOONSHINE

If a friendly host claps you on the back and offers you a shot of his or her home-made *rakija*, think of a good excuse. Drinking local moonshine can (and does occasionally) have serious consequences and can certainly leave you with a very bad hangover. But be tactful, as a downright refusal is very rude.

DO AVOID SENSITIVE SUBJECTS

Some topics of conversation are best avoided. Catholicism and Croatia are sacred areas. Never get Croatia and Yugoslavia (or the Balkans!) mixed up, and try not to point out perceived similarities between Croatians and their near neighbours. Always respect local knowledge and sensibilities.